TRUTH
FOR
ALL
TIME

LIEVE IN GOD THE
HEAVEN AND EART
IN JESUS CHRIST, HI   SON,
LORD:
WAS CONCEIVED BY   GHOST,
N OF THE **VIRGIN MARY**:
FERED UNDER PONTIUS PILATE; WAS
CIFIED, DEAD, AND BURIED: HE DESCENDED
HELL:
THIRD DAY HE ROSE AGAIN FROM THE DEAD:
ASCENDED INTO HEAVEN, AND SITTETH AT
RIGHT HAND OF GOD THE FATHER ALMIGHTY
M THENCE HE SHALL COME TO JUDGE THE
K AND THE DEAD:
IEVE IN THE HOLY GHOST:
HOLY CATHOLIC CHURCH: THE COMMUNION
AINTS:
FORGIVENESS OF SINS:
RESURRECTION OF THE BODY:
THE LIFE EVERLASTING.
N.

I Believe...

The Apostles' Creed
simply explained

Timothy Cross

DayOne

© Day One Publications 2010
First printed 2010

ISBN 978–1–84625–201–3

British Library Cataloguing in Publication Data available

Published by Day One Publications
Ryelands Road, Leominster, HR6 8NZ
☎ 01568 613 740 FAX 01568 611 473
email—sales@dayone.co.uk
web site—www.dayone.co.uk
North American—e-mail—sales@dayonebookstore.com
North American—web site—www.dayonebookstore.com

Cover design by Wayne McMaster
Printed by Orchard Press, Tewkesbury

Commendations

Timothy Cross has a passion for making truth both interesting and infectious. This exploration of the Apostles' Creed is an example of his love for the Bible and his desire to make it relevant to today's generation. I thoroughly recommend this volume.

Dr Derek W. H. Thomas, Professor of Theology, Reformed Theological Seminary, Jackson, USA.

The Apostles' Creed is one of the forgotten treasures of the church. Once known by almost every Christian and recited regularly in almost every church, it is now at best neglected and at worst unknown. Yet this great summary of the essence of the Bible's teaching has been the guardian of what constitutes true Christianity since the days of the Church Fathers. Dr Cross has done today's church an enormous service by providing this re-introduction to the Creed in a way that is both accessible and warmly applied. It is guaranteed to surprise in the best possible way.

Revd Mark Johnston, Grove Chapel, London, England.

Contents

1. I believe in God, the Father almighty, Maker of heaven and earth:
2. And in Jesus Christ, his only begotten Son, our Lord:
3. Who was conceived by the Holy Ghost, born of the Virgin Mary:
4. Suffered under Pontius Pilate; was crucified, dead and buried: he descended into hell:
5. The third day he rose again from the dead:
6. He ascended into heaven, and sitteth at the right hand of God the Father almighty:
7. From thence he shall come to judge the quick and the dead:
8. I believe in the Holy Ghost:
9. The holy catholic church: the communion of saints:
10. The forgiveness of sins:
11. The resurrection of the body:
12. And the life everlasting. Amen.

The Apostles' Creed is one of the clearest and most succinct written distillations of the Christian faith ever penned. Its twelve brief lines encapsulate 'the whole counsel of God' (Acts 20:27) and crystallize the very essence of 'the faith which was once for all delivered to the saints' (Jude 3). Its dealing with primary, as opposed to secondary, truth explains its wide acceptance in the Christian church from her early days until the present. Here is a Statement of Faith on which all Christians are agreed. Here is a truly 'ecumenical' Statement of Faith, one concerned solely with what is essential—as opposed to peripheral—to biblical Christianity.

Surprisingly, the exact origins of the Apostles' Creed are unknown. Its earliest historical mention is in a letter written by the Council of Milan in AD 390. Yet it is thought to have originated as early as the second century AD—just half a century after the death of the apostle John, Christ's 'beloved disciple'.

Just why the Apostles' Creed was written is also unknown. The consensus, though, is that a short statement of Christian fundamentals was needed for converts to the Christian faith to repeat before they were baptized. Hence 'I believe …'—a personal confession of faith as well as of objective truths. The creed may also have developed to counteract heresy, for false teaching can be refuted by affirming the truth. Consequently, a statement of truth becomes a yardstick against which error can be measured, revealing where a doctrine is contrary to and deviates from the teaching of Scripture.

It would be nice to think that the twelve lines of the Apostles' Creed can be explained by each one of the twelve apostles of Christ contributing a line each. This, though, was not the case—later legends apart. The term 'Apostles' Creed' refers to the apostolic doctrine of the creed, not to the apostolic composition of the creed. Although this creed cannot claim to be apostolic in authorship, it certainly summarizes the fundamental, primary truths of the Christian faith as taught and proclaimed by the apostles of Christ. Hence its invaluable use in giving us a firm grounding in Christian fundamentals; '… built on the foundation of the apostles and prophets, Christ Jesus Himself being the chief cornerstone' (Eph. 2:20).

The first-century church was composed of people who believed certain truths: 'they continued steadfastly in the apostles' doctrine ...' (Acts 2:42); 'nourished in the words of faith and of the good doctrine' (1 Tim. 4:6). Today's twenty-first-century Christians should also know what they believe and why, and what it is that particularly distinguishes the Christian faith. In the good providence of God, the Apostles' Creed has been bequeathed to the church as a means to this end.

Timothy Cross
Cardiff
Wales

The one true God

I believe in God, the Father almighty, Maker of heaven and earth ...

T he Christian faith begins, continues and ends with God—the one true God who made the universe; the one true and living God as revealed in his Word, the Bible; the one true God who, as this creed states, is triune in nature and thus worshipped as Father, Son and Holy Spirit.

The goal of the Christian faith is the glory and praise of this one true God. Even the blessing of humanity is subservient to this one overriding and overarching purpose. The Christian faith—in complete contrast to the ethos of the world—is distinctly and definitely theo-centric. It is God-centred, God-focused, God-occupied and God-preoccupied. 'But the LORD is the true God; He is the living God and the everlasting King' (Jer. 10:10). A true Christian looks to God—'I believe in God ...'—the fount of all blessing and the source of all existence. True Christianity is characterized by a resolute and robust faith in God—in his grace, his promises, his providence—and in God alone. The motto of true Christianity is 'Soli Deo Gloria'—to God alone be the glory.

I believe in God

Affirming our faith in God raises the question: Can Almighty God really be known? Surely he is above and beyond us? The Christian answer is that God can indeed be known. This is because he has condescended to make himself known. He would be unknowable had he not chosen graciously to reveal himself. The Christian faith affirms that God has actually revealed himself, for he has given us both a general and a special revelation of himself in both his world and his Word. Through these we can both know about him and even come to know him personally.

GOD'S WORLD

If we would deny the existence of God, we would first have to deny the existence of the world. Creation is inexplicable without 'God ... Maker of heaven and earth'. 'For since the creation of the world His invisible attributes are clearly seen, being understood by the things that are made, even His eternal power and Godhead, so that they are without excuse' (Rom. 1:20). Viewing the skies, the oceans, the mountains and the stars we glimpse something of the divine might, immensity, intelligence and beauty. They tell us something about the God who made them.

The heavens declare the glory of God;
And the firmament shows His handiwork.
Day unto day utters speech,
And night unto night reveals knowledge.   (Ps. 19:1–2)

Yet God's general revelation in the natural world has its limitations. The computer on which I type obviously has a maker. I sense that that maker is highly intelligent, but I don't know him or her personally. I would, though, if he or she came and spoke to me. The Christian faith makes the amazing claim that the God behind the universe has indeed spoken. The Christian faith is a religion of the Word—God's Word. It claims that God has made himself known as he has given us his Word.

GOD'S WORD

Words are the verbal articulation of the thoughts of our minds. Amazingly, the Christian faith asserts that Almighty God has actually revealed to us the thoughts of his mind. He has given us his Word. The sixty-six books which constitute the Bible are the written Word of God. Hence, if we would know God, we have to read the Bible—the Book which alone reveals the otherwise invisible, unknowable God. 'All Scripture is given by inspiration of God ...' (2 Tim. 3:16); that is, 'all Scripture is God-breathed' (NIV).

The Christian faith is founded and grounded on the sure Word of God. God, by his Holy Spirit, revealed his Word to the various human authors of the Bible. His divine superintendence ensured that they wrote down accurately what he wanted them and us to know, and preserved it for posterity: '... the word of our God stands forever' (Isa. 40:8). It is from this divine inspiration of the Holy Scriptures that the inerrancy, authority, vitality and incomparability of the Bible flow.

How precious is the book divine,
By inspiration given;
Bright as a lamp its doctrines shine
To guide our souls to heaven.   (John Fawcett, 1782)

Knowing God and knowing the Bible, then, are inseparable. 'The Word of God, which is contained in the Scriptures of the Old and New Testaments, is the only rule to direct us how we may glorify and enjoy him' (*Westminster Shorter Catechism* (WSC), Q. 2). The central message of the Bible is encapsulated in one verse, John 3:16, which states, 'For God so loved the world that He gave His only begotten Son, that whoever believes in Him should not perish but have everlasting life.'

God and his Word are inseparable when it comes to knowing God. We can, though, go a step further and state that God's Word—his revelation—and Jesus Christ are also inseparable. One is the Word in print, the other is the Word in person. As the Bible is God's inspired Word, so the Lord Jesus Christ is God's incarnate Word. He is God in human flesh. In the Christ of the Bible we have the unsurpassed and unsurpassable revelation of the one true God. 'No one has seen God at any time. The only begotten Son, who is in the bosom of the Father, He has declared Him' (John 1:18).

In Jesus, Almighty God 'came down to our level' and actually revealed himself in a real, human person. Jesus is '"Immanuel", which is translated, "God with us"' (Matt. 1:23). He once went as far as to make the awesome claim that 'He who has seen Me has seen the Father' (John 14:9).

So, in summary, we can know God because God has made himself known to us. In his Word, the Bible, we may hear God's voice; and God's written Word, the Bible, directs us to God's living Word, the Lord Jesus Christ, for at a particular moment in world history 'the Word became flesh and dwelt among us, and we beheld His glory, the glory as of the only begotten of the Father, full of grace and truth' (John 1:14). We do not have to speculate as to what God might be like, as in the Bible we have his own divine revelation. What is God like? He is Christ-like. The special and unique Christian way of knowing and addressing God, however, is by using the intimate term 'Father'.

I believe in God, the Father almighty

My Father is omnipotent,
And that you can't deny;
A God of might and miracles,
'Tis written in the sky;
The Bible tells us of His power
And wisdom all way through;
And every little bird and flower
Are testimonies too.   (John W. Peterson, 1921–2006, 'It Took a Miracle')

The term 'Father' refers to the first Person of the divine Trinity. It speaks of God's authority, affection and wisdom.

HIS AUTHORITY

God's description as 'Father' reminds us of his authority. Biblical society was patriarchal. The father was the head of the household. Almighty God is the ultimate authority. He is the 'Most High' (Ps. 92:1), and as such is to be revered and obeyed.

HIS AFFECTION

The description 'Father' also speaks of the mutual affection which exists between God and his children. A good father loves his children and always wants the very best for them. His children know this and love and trust him in return. Human fathers, of course, have their failings. God the Father, though, cannot fail. His goodness is unalloyed, his power infinite and his love immeasurable. 'As a father pities his children, so the LORD pities those who fear Him' (Ps. 103:13). 'If you then, being evil, know how to give good gifts to your children, how much more will your Father who is in heaven give good things to those who ask Him!' (Matt. 7:11).

HIS WISDOM

Describing God as 'Father' also reminds us of his wisdom. Children look to their parents for advice and guidance, for their greater years give them greater experience and wisdom. The eternal God is infinite in wisdom. Omniscience is one of his attributes—'Great is our Lord, and mighty in power; His understanding is infinite' (Ps. 147:5).

KNOWING GOD AS 'FATHER'

Knowing and addressing God as 'Father'—with all its consequences, connotations and implications—is a distinctive and distinguishing privilege of Christians. Christians both submit to God's fatherly authority and revel in his fatherly love. Paul began most of his letters with the opening signature tune 'Grace to you and peace from God our Father and the Lord Jesus Christ' (Eph. 1:2, for example). Jesus said to his disciples, 'In this manner, therefore, pray: Our *Father* in heaven …' (Matt. 6:9).[1]

Addressing the God of the universe as 'Father' and being in an intimate child–parent relationship with him is only possible by God's grace—his gracious initiative in adopting us into his family. According to the Bible, not everyone can know and address God as 'Father'—only Christians, who have been born again by God's Spirit into God's family. 'Adoption'—that is, adoption into God's family—is one of the many synonyms the Bible uses to describe Christian salvation. By nature we are sinners—children of wrath, outside God's family, separated from God. By God's grace in Christ, we become the children of God—reconciled to him, brought into his household, under his fatherly love and care, never to be cast out. 'Adoption is an act of God's free grace, whereby we are received into the number, and have a right to all the privileges, of the sons of God' (*WSC*, Q. 34).

The wonder of knowing God as Father never grows stale. The aged apostle John—by this point a Christian of long standing—exclaimed, 'Behold, what manner of love the Father has bestowed on us, that we should be called children of God!' (1 John 3:1). By God's grace, in Christ, Christians have become God's intimates. We have access to him in prayer. We know him as our loving Father in heaven. We may tap into his love, wisdom and power. He is 'God, the Father *almighty*'. Nothing is too difficult for our heavenly Father. He has the answer to all our difficulties and he will send us his grace to cope with all our burdens and problems.

The Apostles' Creed, then, begins by affirming, 'I believe in God, the Father almighty'. That our Father is truly 'all-mighty' is evidenced from his being the 'Maker of heaven and earth'.

Maker of heaven and earth

According to the Bible, the existence of the universe cannot be divorced from the existence of God. The universe exists because God exists. He created it; it is inexplicable without him. Scripture teaches divine creation: 'In the beginning God created the heavens and the earth' (Gen. 1:1).

By the word of the LORD the heavens were made,
And all the host of them by the breath of His mouth.
He gathers the waters of the sea together as a heap;
He lays up the deep in storehouses.
Let all the earth fear the LORD,
Let all the inhabitants of the world stand in awe of Him.
For He spoke, and it was done;
He commanded, and it stood fast.

(Ps. 33:6–9)

God's creation of the world in six days, merely by speaking it into existence, is proof that he is indeed 'God, the Father almighty'. He is the Originator of all things. He is infinite in power and wisdom. Nothing is too difficult for him to achieve. With Job, we can say to God, 'I know that You can do everything, and that no purpose of Yours can be withheld from You' (Job 42:2). Jeremiah the prophet exclaimed similarly, 'Ah, Lord GOD! Behold, You have made the heavens and the earth by Your great power and outstretched arm. There is nothing too hard for You' (Jer. 32:17).

The fact that God our Father created the universe has certain pastoral implications for his people. Scripture teaches that this Almighty God actually disposes his power for the benefit, blessing and help of his people. In the Psalms we read, 'My help comes from the LORD, who made heaven and earth' (Ps. 121:2), and 'Our help is in the name of the LORD, who made heaven and earth' (Ps. 124:8). Such verses are written for our encouragement. They remind us that, while our difficulties and problems are great to us—sometimes seemingly insurmountable—they are nothing to Almighty God our Father. We may thus turn to our loving Father in heaven and bring our problems and burdens to him, knowing that with him, as our heavenly Father, there is infinite mercy and, as the Creator of the universe, infinite might. Matthew Henry, the famous Bible commentator, wrote,

We must encourage our confidence in God with this: 'He made heaven and earth.' And he who did that can do anything. He made the world out of nothing, himself alone, by a word's speaking, in a little time, and 'all very good', very excellent and very beautiful; and therefore, however great our difficulties and inadequacies are, he has power sufficient for our support, assistance, help and relief.[2]

And so the Apostles' Creed begins by affirming both the Fatherhood of God and his creative majesty. By faith, the Christian affirms, 'I believe in God, the Father almighty, Maker of heaven and earth.'

Notes

1 All italics in Scripture quotations has been added for emphasis.
2 **Matthew Henry,** *Matthew Henry's Commentary on the Whole Bible*, vol. 3 (Peabody, MA: Hendrickson, 1991), p. 594.

The Person of Christ

And in Jesus Christ, his only begotten Son, our Lord …

Acts 11:26 informs us that 'the disciples were first called *Christians* in Antioch'. The term 'Christian' means 'Christ's one'. A Christian is one who belongs to Jesus. Christianity is Christ. The Christian faith is not a creed or a particular manner of life—important though both of these are to the Christian faith. Primarily, the Christian faith is occupied and preoccupied with the Person and Work of the Lord Jesus Christ: who he is and what he came to earth to do. It is the Lord Jesus Christ who is the object of the Christian's faith. It is the Lord Jesus Christ who is praised and extolled in Christian hymns. It is the Lord Jesus Christ who is preached in Christian sermons. It is the Lord Jesus Christ who is the key that unlocks the Bible. It is the Lord Jesus Christ who is the focal point of the two Christian sacraments of baptism and the Lord's Supper. Christianity is Christ. This line of the Apostles' Creed focuses our attention on his blessed Person. 'Jesus Christ' is described here as 'his' (that is, God the Father's) 'only begotten Son, our Lord'. Let us now unpack this succinct statement.

The Saviour's name

JESUS

'Jesus' is the human name given from heaven to the Son of God when he came to earth. The name 'Jesus' is the Greek translation of the Hebrew 'Joshua'. It means 'The Lord saves'; 'you shall call His name JESUS, for He will save His people from their sins' (Matt. 1:21). This shows us that there is no watertight division between the Person and the Work of Christ. Who he is, is inextricably bound up with what he came to earth to do. In Bible times, names and natures were believed to be much more closely tied than they are today. Jesus's name thus gives him away. He is the Saviour of sinners. He said of himself, 'the Son of Man has come to seek and to save that which was lost' (Luke 19:10).

The human name of Jesus reminds us of the historicity of the Christian faith. Jesus is both a historical and a historic figure. The Christian faith is based on fact, not fiction; history, not mythology. The birth of Jesus has actually divided history into two eras—BC and AD. We thus prove the historical reality of the Christian faith—that is, that it concerns facts which actually happened in time and space—every time we write the year on our letters.

'Jesus' is the human name that was given to the very Son of God. It means 'Saviour'.

There is no name so sweet on earth,
No name so sweet in heaven,
The Name, before His wondrous birth,
To Christ the Saviour given.

We love to sing of Christ our King,
And hail Him, blessed Jesus!
For there's no word ear ever heard
So dear, so sweet as 'Jesus'!   (George W. Bethune, 1858)

The Saviour's title

CHRIST

'Christ' is not a surname but a title. Compare 'Charles Mountbatten-Windsor' with 'Prince Charles'. The title 'Christ' means 'the anointed one'. It is the Greek word for the Hebrew 'Messiah'.

In Old Testament times, God, through his prophets, promised to send his own special agent into the world—One who would bring in the blessed kingdom of heaven. How the Jews longed for this special agent! How they longed for God's Messiah! In Jesus, the promises of God were fulfilled. He is the Christ of God. A milestone in the Gospel records occurred when Peter, having witnessed both the words and works of Jesus first-hand for some time, was forced to confess to him, 'You are the Christ, the Son of the living God' (Matt. 16:16). Truly 'all the promises of God in Him are Yes, and in Him Amen' (2 Cor. 1:20).

In Old Testament times, prophets, priests and kings were all anointed with oil at the outset of their respective ministries. This symbolized their being set apart by God for service and endowed with his Holy Spirit, to enable them to fulfil the specific roles and spheres of service to which they had been called.

At the outset of his earthly ministry, Jesus—*the* Anointed One—was likewise specifically endowed with the Holy Spirit. Jesus commenced his ministry by being baptized in the river Jordan. Matthew relates that, when Jesus was baptized, 'He saw the Spirit of God descending like a dove and alighting upon Him' (Matt. 3:16). As *the* Christ—*the* Anointed One— Jesus fulfils the threefold role of prophet, priest and king in his one blessed Person:

Christ executeth the office of a prophet, in revealing to us, by his word and Spirit, the will of God for our salvation.

Christ executeth the office of a priest, in his once offering up of himself a sacrifice to satisfy divine justice, and reconcile us to God, and in making continual intercession for us.

Christ executeth the office of a king, in subduing us to himself, in ruling and defending us, and in restraining and conquering all his and our enemies.   (*WSC, Q. 24–26*).

Jesus, then, is the *Christ*—God's Anointed One.

Hail to the Lord's Anointed,
Great David's greater Son!
Hail, in the time appointed,
His reign on earth begun!
He comes to break oppression,
To set the captive free,
To take away transgression,
And rule in equity.   (James Montgomery, 1821)

The Saviour's identity

THE ONLY BEGOTTEN SON

The Christian faith cannot be separated from the personal identity of the One who lies at its centre. The Christian faith depends on the identity of Jesus Christ—simply who he is. Our line of the creed here—derived squarely from Scripture—describes Jesus as 'his' (that is, God the Father's) 'only begotten Son'. Here we see the uniqueness and the incomparability of the Lord Jesus Christ.

We saw in the previous chapter that 'adoption' is one of the synonyms for Christian salvation: in Christ, God adopts sinners into his family and gives them the status of the sons of God. 'But as many as received Him, to them He gave the right to become children of God, to those who believe in His name' (John 1:12). The Sonship of Christ, however, is infinitely different from Christian sonship. Christ is the 'only begotten Son' of God. His Sonship is not adoptive but eternal and intrinsic. He has always been the Son of God. He is the Son of God and God the Son. Here we are drawn into the mystery of the divine Trinity which is part of the 'warp and woof' of the Apostles' Creed and the touchstone of Christian orthodoxy. According to the creed—and according to the Scriptures from which the creed is drawn—the one true God exists—and has existed eternally—in three Persons of God the Father, Son and Holy Spirit. Jesus is the Second Person of the Trinity. He has always existed as the Son of God, even though there was a moment in time when he took upon himself human flesh and entered our world of time and space which he had been instrumental in making. 'In the beginning was the Word ... All things were made through Him ... And the Word became flesh' (John 1:1, 3, 14). The uniqueness of the Christian faith, then, stems from the uniqueness of Christ's identity. He is the eternal Son of God. He is the 'only begotten Son' of God.

To describe oneself as the unique and only Son of God would be blasphemy were it not actually true. That Jesus knew himself to be the unique Son of God is patent from Scripture. His divine Sonship was part of his self-understanding and self-identity. The earliest recorded words which we have of Jesus come from the time of his childhood. As a child, in the temple at Jerusalem, he explained to his earthly parents, Mary and

Joseph, 'Did you not know that I must be about My Father's business?' (Luke 2:49). Then Mark relates that, at the end of Jesus's earthly ministry, when he was on trial and under oath, 'the high priest asked Him, saying to Him, "Are You the Christ, the Son of the Blessed?" Jesus said, "I am. And you will see the Son of Man sitting at the right hand of the Power, and coming with the clouds of heaven." Then the high priest tore his clothes and said, "What further need do we have of witnesses? You have heard the blasphemy! ..."' (Mark 14:61–64). It is doubtful whether those who say that Jesus never claimed to be the Son of God have ever read the Bible. It was Jesus's own assertion of his divine Sonship which condemned him to the cruel death on the cross. Jesus, however, could only speak the truth. He knew himself to be the eternal Son of God, and could only say so. In his 'High Priestly prayer' to his Father, he betrayed his eternality and pre-existence when he mentioned 'the glory which I had with You before the world was' (John 17:5).

The incomparability of the Christian faith flows from Jesus's identity as God's 'only begotten Son'. He is the Son of God and God the Son, co-equal with the Father and the Holy Spirit, with whom he dwelt and with whom he dwells in the unity of the Holy Trinity.

The Saviour's deity

OUR LORD

The statement 'Jesus is Lord' is believed to be the earliest ever Christian creed and confession of faith. It is a statement which lost many Christians their lives in the days of the early church. In the first century, the Roman Emperor was deified. Christians, however, were unable to make the confession 'Caesar is Lord' as they knew that 'Jesus is Lord'. Their refusal to bow down to Caesar often led to their martyrdom—to their being thrown to the lions.

The title 'LORD' is used of God himself in the Old Testament. In Isaiah 43:11, for instance, God himself states, 'I, even I, am the LORD, and besides Me there is no saviour.' In applying the title of 'Lord' to Jesus, then, the New Testament betrays his deity.

The absolute deity of Christ—that is, his 'God-ness' and co-equality with God the Father and God the Holy Spirit—is one of the fundamentals of the Christian faith. Those who deny that Jesus is anything less than 'Mighty God' (Isa. 9:6) cannot be termed 'Christian' in the biblical sense. Scripture affirms the absolute deity of Christ right through its pages; 'yet for us there is one God, the Father, of whom are all things, and we for Him; and one Lord Jesus Christ, through whom are all things, and through whom we live' (1 Cor. 8:6).

The deity of Christ is part of the very fabric of the New Testament—it is not a matter of the occasional 'proof text'. Plain statements concerning Christ's deity are certainly there in the Bible, however. John 1:1, for instance, affirms, 'In the beginning was the Word, and the Word was with God, and the Word was God.' Colossians 2:9 states that 'in Him dwells all the fullness of the Godhead bodily'.

Did Jesus himself consider himself to be divine, though? Yes, he did. In Exodus 3:14 God revealed his name to Moses as the great 'I AM WHO I AM'. And Jesus frequently applied this name to himself in his various 'I am' sayings. In John 10:11, for instance, Jesus said, 'I am the good shepherd', while in Psalm 23:1 we read that 'The LORD is my shepherd'. Jesus was thus affirming his deity.

THE WORKS OF JESUS

Jesus's deity is also proved by what he did, as well as by what he said. Jesus performed many miracles. Such miracles as his healing the sick, raising the dead, calming the stormy Sea of Galilee at a word, making a fig-tree wither at once, feeding five thousand with five loaves and two fish, turning water into wine, and others, are part of the very texture of the historical Gospel records. They were works of compassion for sure, but they also evidence Jesus's deity; they are, as John's Gospel terms them, 'signs'. Jesus said of them, 'the works which the Father has given Me to finish—the very works that I do—bear witness of Me, that the Father has sent Me' (John 5:36).

Jesus's conquest of the grave—his resurrection—is usually seen as the final linch-pin proving his deity. He is the Lord of life and death. He defeated death. He was 'declared to be the Son of God with power according to the Spirit of holiness, by the resurrection from the dead' (Rom. 1:4).

A basic biblical axiom is that God alone is to be worshipped. Worshipping anyone or anything other than the one true God is condemned as idolatry. John's Gospel climaxes with Thomas worshipping the Lord Jesus Christ. The risen Christ appeared to him and the other disciples in the Upper Room. He showed them the scars from his crucifixion. Then 'Thomas answered and said to Him, "My Lord and my God!"' (John 20:28). Jesus did not rebuke Thomas for idolatry. He accepted the worship given to him—just as he continues to accept the worship given to him from the church militant on earth and the church triumphant in heaven.

Christians worship Christ as the Son of God and God the Son. They rejoice in him as their Saviour. They own him collectively as 'our Lord'. There is none like him. 'Jesus Christ is Lord' (Phil. 2:11)—'Jesus Christ, his only begotten Son, our Lord'.

Join all the glorious names
Of wisdom, love and power,
That mortals ever knew,
That angels ever bore;
All are to mean to speak His worth,
Too poor to set my Saviour forth.

(Isaac Watts, 1709)

The birth of Christ

Jesus Christ ... Who was conceived by the Holy Ghost, born of the Virgin Mary ...

The third line of the Apostles' Creed draws our attention to the incarnation of the 'only begotten Son' of God; that is, it is concerned with Christ's becoming man 'for us men and for our salvation' (*Nicene Creed*). Specifically, it focuses on his conception at Nazareth and his birth at Bethlehem. Christ's birth was a natural one, whereas his conception was a supernatural one. His birth was normal, but his conception was not. Scripture is clear that he was conceived miraculously, without a human father. Scripture teaches that he was conceived by the miraculous agency and instrumentality of the Holy Spirit, in the womb of the Virgin Mary: 'Christ, the Son of God, became man, by taking to himself a true body, and a reasonable soul, being conceived by the power of the Holy Ghost, in the womb of the Virgin Mary, and born of her, yet without sin' (*WSC, Q. 22*).

An epochal milestone in history

The conception and birth of Christ is a milestone of human, world and salvation history in a category all its own. It contains many paradoxes which fuel our praise. In Christ, the eternal entered into time. In Christ, the uncreated Creator entered his creation. In Christ, God became man. In Christ, the Son of God became a son of man, so the sons of men might become the sons of God. A sinless One was born so that sinners might be born again. He came to earth so that we might go at last to heaven. He became poor so that we might be enriched by his grace: 'you know the grace of our Lord Jesus Christ, that though He was rich, yet for your sakes He became poor, that you through His poverty might become rich' (2 Cor. 8:9). The immortal Son of God took on himself our mortality so that mortal sinners might be raised to immortality. He was born to die—and in dying to procure our salvation—so that dying sinners might have eternal life through faith in him.

We come, then, to the incarnation of the eternal Son of God. This epochal moment in world history and the saga of redemption was 'inscripturated' by John in the Prologue to his Gospel when he wrote, 'And the Word became flesh and dwelt among us, and we beheld His glory, the glory as of the only begotten of the Father, full of grace and truth' (John 1:14).

But lo! He leaves those heavenly forms;
The Word descends and dwells in clay,
That I Ie may converse hold with worms,
Dressed in such feeble flesh as they.

(Isaac Watts, 1674–1748,
'Before the Heavens Were Spread Abroad')

The divine conception

WHO WAS CONCEIVED BY THE HOLY GHOST

Christ's 'virginal conception' by the Holy Spirit was not a miracle that came out of the blue but was rather a key part of God's carefully orchestrated, predestined redemption plan. Some seven hundred years previous to Jesus's conception, God had prophesied through Isaiah the prophet that this would be his Son's particular mode of entry into the universe. Isaiah 7:14 reads, 'Behold, the virgin shall conceive and bear a son, and shall call His name Immanuel.' Going back further than Isaiah, back even to the very dawn of human history, we see that in Eden's garden, God promised that a coming 'seed of a woman' would, in the fullness of time, bruise Satan's head, thus undoing the ravages which sin and Satan had wrought (see the first ever gospel promise, the *protoeuangelion*, in Gen. 3:15). Both of these prophecies and promises found their fulfilment in Christ when he was 'conceived by the Holy Ghost [or Spirit]' in Mary's womb, so that he could live, die and procure the salvation of God's people. It was, then, 'for us men and for our salvation [that he] came down from heaven, and was incarnate by the Holy Ghost of the Virgin Mary, and was made man' (*Nicene Creed*).

Two of the Gospel writers lay special stress on Christ's 'virgin birth'.

MATTHEW'S GOSPEL

Matthew relates that Joseph, Mary's husband-to-be, was in turmoil when he first found out that his bride-to-be was expecting a baby. He thought the worst. It seemed that his marriage was over before it had begun. Matthew 1:20, however, reports that, 'while he thought about these things, behold, an angel of the Lord appeared to him in a dream, saying, "Joseph, son of David, do not be afraid to take to you Mary your wife, for that which is conceived in her is of the Holy Spirit"'. A little earlier, Matthew had written, as a matter of unembellished fact, that 'After … Mary was betrothed to Joseph, before they came together, she was found with child of the Holy Spirit' (Matt. 1:18).

Matthew's Gospel, then, is crystal clear: Christ was conceived by the Holy Spirit. He was virgin-born. Similarly with …

LUKE'S GOSPEL

It is likely that 'Luke the beloved physician' (Col. 4:14) obtained his information concerning Christ's virginal conception from Mary herself. He would have had her confidence ('in the surgery', as it were) when he researched his Gospel. Luke records Mary's initial perplexity. She knew that children could not be conceived without there being two parties, a male and a female. As she was, as yet, unmarried, and was obedient to God's law, the conception of a child was humanly impossible. She, like Joseph, also received an angelic explanation. God was going to perform a miracle: 'And the angel … said to her, "The Holy Spirit will come upon you, and the power of the Highest will overshadow you; therefore, also, that Holy One who is to be born will be called the Son of God"' (Luke 1:35).

The importance of the virgin birth

For the past two thousand years, unbelievers have slandered Christ's virgin birth. Sceptics have decried and continue to deride it. Christians, however, believe it. We do so because the Bible tells us so. And we do so because we know that 'with God nothing will be impossible' (Luke 1:37). Belief in 'God, the Father almighty' entails belief in the miraculous.

The inclusion of Christ's virginal conception in the Apostles' Creed shows that it is considered to be one of the essential, non-negotiable articles of the Christian faith. This is so because Christ's virgin birth is bound up with his sinlessness—his impeccability. 'Christ Jesus came into the world to save sinners' (1 Tim. 1:15), and only a sinless one is qualified to save sinners. Only a sinless one could offer up his life as an atoning sacrifice on behalf of the sins of others.

Scripture attests to Christ's complete sinlessness. Hebrews 7:26 describes him as being 'holy, harmless, undefiled, separate from sinners'. Had Christ been conceived through the normal instrumentality of a human father, he would have inherited our human sin, and hence would have been disqualified from being our Saviour. All people since Adam are born sinners. Sin is passed on through natural generation: 'through one man [Adam] sin entered the world, and death through sin, and thus death spread to all men, because all sinned …' (Rom. 5:12).

In Christ, 'the last Adam', God did 'a new thing'. Christ's conception was not by the agency of a fallen, human man, but by the instrumentality of the Holy Spirit of God—the third Person of the Trinity. He was 'conceived by the Holy Ghost'. And he had to be, if he was to be our sinless Saviour. Unlike every other human being, Christ was born with a sinless nature. He alone could not sin. He 'knew no sin' (2 Cor. 5:21), 'committed no sin' (1 Peter 2:22) 'and in Him there is no sin' (1 John 3:5). Note, then, the vital importance of Christ's virgin conception. Here is no peripheral matter. Its truth affects our eternal salvation. John Calvin wrote of Christ, 'He was a true man, like us in everything, with the single exception of sin … He was Himself conceived in the womb of the Virgin, by the marvellous and inexpressible power of the Holy Spirit, so as to be born without being tainted by any fleshly corruption, but sanctified by sovereign purity.'[1]

The divine birth

BORN OF THE VIRGIN MARY

Nine months after his supernatural conception, 'Jesus was born in Bethlehem of Judea in the days of Herod the king' (Matt. 2:1). Christ's birth in Bethlehem—rather than Nazareth, Mary's home-town—was again in fulfilment of prophecy. Seven hundred years previously, God had prophesied through Micah the prophet that Bethlehem would be the location of the Messiah's birth (see Micah 5:2). But what a moment it was when Mary 'brought forth her firstborn Son, and wrapped Him in swaddling cloths, and laid Him in a manger' (Luke 2:7)! So momentous was this birth that it split time into events recorded before and after its occurrence. For Christ's birth split history into the eras BC and AD. The news of Christ's birth was first broadcast to some humble shepherds who were going about their business in the fields surrounding the town of Bethlehem. An angel of the Lord proclaimed to them, 'there is born to you this day in the city of David a Savior, who is Christ the Lord' (Luke 2:11). Fittingly, the skies were then filled with angelic praise, for 'suddenly there was with the angel a multitude of the heavenly host praising God and saying: "Glory to God in the highest, and on earth peace, goodwill toward men"' (Luke 2:13–14).

The sending of his own Son into the world to save sinners is indeed the crowning expression of the divine goodwill. The sending of his own Son into the world to save sinners is the unmatched and unmatchable expression of God's grace—that is, his love to the undeserving and ill-deserving. It is a 'fact of the faith' which is celebrated by Christians today just as it has been celebrated by Christians for the past two thousand years.

The *Heidelberg Catechism* asks, 'What profit dost thou receive by Christ's holy conception and nativity?' It answers, 'That He is our Mediator; and with His innocence and perfect holiness, covers in the sight of God, my sins, wherein I was conceived and brought forth' (Q. 36). More poetically, Charles Wesley, meditating upon the fact that Christ was 'conceived by the Holy Ghost, born of the Virgin Mary', penned the following well-known lines:

Christ, by highest heaven adored,
Christ, the everlasting Lord;
Late in time, behold Him come,
Offspring of a virgin's womb.
Veiled in flesh the Godhead see;
Hail the incarnate Deity!
Pleased as Man with men to dwell,
Jesus, our Immanuel.   (Charles Wesley, 'Hark! The Herald Angels Sing', 1739)

Note

1   **John Calvin** (trans. **Stuart Olyott**), *Truth for all Time* (Edinburgh: Banner of Truth, 1998), p. 39.

The Passion of Christ

[He] Suffered under Pontius Pilate; was crucified, dead and buried: he descended into hell ...

It is striking that the Apostles' Creed goes straight from Christ's birth at Bethlehem to his death at Calvary thirty-three years later, giving no mention of the remarkable life which he lived in-between. In doing this, the creed is squarely in line with Scripture, for the stress of Scripture is not on Christ's life but his death. In the Bible, all roads lead to the cross of Calvary, for it was at Calvary that Christ actually procured the eternal salvation of his people. The sinner's salvation is gained, not so much from Christ's living, teaching, miracles or example, but from his dying.

The cross of Calvary—that is, Christ's finished work of redemption—lies at the centre of the centre of the Christian faith and the heart of the heart of the biblical revelation. The cross of Christ is prefigured and prophesied in the Old Testament, described in the Gospels—the four Gospels have, in fact, been described as four Passion narratives with extended introductions—preached in Acts and explained in the epistles. It is the cross of Christ which is depicted visually in the Christian sacraments of baptism and the Lord's Supper. And it is the cross of Christ which is the sum and substance of the Christian gospel: 'we preach Christ crucified' (1 Cor. 1:23). The aim of Christian evangelism is, under God, to bring sinners to the foot of the cross and to trust in the One who there gave his life as an atoning sacrifice for sinners.

The cross of Christ, therefore, could not be more central or crucial to the Christian faith. There is no salvation which by-passes the cross. The redeemed in heaven continue to extol the glories of the cross and the worth and wonder of the Crucified: 'You are worthy ... for You were slain, and have redeemed us to God by Your blood' (Rev. 5:9). Hence the Apostles' Creed has good, scriptural warrant for moving straight from Christ's cradle to his cross—his incarnation to his immolation, his first breath to his redeeming blood, from Bethlehem to Calvary.

We may not know, we cannot tell,
What pains He had to bear,
But we believe it was for us
He hung and suffered there.

He died that we might be forgiven,
He died to make us good,
That we might go at last to heaven,
Saved by His precious blood.

(Cecil Frances Alexander,
'There is a Green Hill Far Away', 1848)

Unpacking this very compact line, we note first of all that Christ:

Suffered under Pontius Pilate

This places Christ's death firmly at a particular point in world history, for Pontius Pilate was the Roman governor—or Procurator—of Judea from AD 26–37. The Christian faith is based on historical fact, not cleverly invented fiction. It was Pontius Pilate who gave the final consent that Jesus should be crucified. The Jewish crowd bayed for Jesus's blood—aided and abetted by the Jewish authorities. Yet the Jewish leaders in Roman times had no authority to inflict the death penalty. This was vested in Rome, with Pontius Pilate as its local figurehead. Pilate knew Jesus was innocent of all the charges laid against him, yet he feared the crowd. Afraid that there would be a riot that would cause him to lose his governorship, 'Pilate ... took water and washed his hands before the multitude ... and when he had scourged Jesus, he delivered him to be crucified' (Matt. 27:24, 26).

It is thus true to say that, while the factors and 'players' which caused Jesus's death were many and complex—they included the plan of God, the sin of the world, Judas Iscariot, the Jewish authorities and the Roman soldiers—Jesus could not, and would not, have been crucified were it not for the action and assent of Pontius Pilate. He 'suffered under Pontius Pilate'. Under the sovereignty of God, Pilate condemned Jesus to death so that we might know 'no condemnation' (Rom. 8:1).

As an interesting aside, we also note that Pontius Pilate had an official residence in Caesarea on the coast, as well as in Jerusalem. The headquarters of the Roman garrison was located in Caesarea. In 1961, a stone slab bearing Pontius Pilate's name was discovered at Caesarea, confirming the historicity of the inspired Gospel records.

Next we note that Christ ...

Was crucified

Crucifixion was a cruel and barbaric form of capital punishment invented by the Romans. It entailed the victim being nailed to a plank of wood and hung up to die a long, lingering death by asphyxiation. Crucifixion was always carried out in a prominent, public place. The idea was that it would act as a deterrent to crime. Crucifixion was thus a most horrible mix of both personal excruciation and public humiliation. The emphasis of the Bible, however, is on the spiritual suffering of Christ at Calvary, not on his physical suffering—enormous though the latter undoubtedly was.

Old Testament law stated, 'If a man has committed a sin deserving of death and he is put to death, and you hang him on a tree, his body shall not remain overnight on the tree, but you shall surely bury him that day ... for he who is hanged is accursed of God' (Deut. 21:22–23). Paul gives a 'Christological amplification' of this key verse in Galatians 3:13, taking us to the heart of the meaning of Christ's crucifixion: 'Christ has redeemed us from the curse of the law, having become a curse for us (for it is written, "Cursed is everyone who hangs on a tree").' Paul is saying that at Calvary, Christ was cursed by God so that we might be blessed. He was judged for our sins so that the judgement we deserve for our sins might be removed. He was punished by God so that we might be pardoned by God. At Calvary, God's judgement and mercy met, for Calvary enables God both to condemn sin and pardon the sinner. Christ's death at Calvary was thus a *substitutionary* death. He died in the place of sinners: '... [Christ] who Himself bore our sins in His own body on the tree' (1 Peter 2:24); 'He was wounded for our transgressions' (Isa. 53:5); '... who was delivered up because of our offenses' (Rom. 4:25).

O Love divine! What has Thou done?
The immortal God hath died for me!
The Father's co-eternal Son
Bore all my sins upon the tree.
The immortal God for me hath died;
My Lord, my Love, is crucified!

Is crucified for me and you,
To bring us rebels back to God.
Believe, believe the record true,
Ye now are bought with Jesus' blood.
Pardon for sin flows from His side:
My Lord, my Love, is crucified.   (Charles Wesley, 1707–1788)

Was ... dead

There is no doubt that at Calvary Jesus really died. He was 'obedient to the point of death, even the death of the cross' (Phil. 2:8). Jesus himself viewed his death at Calvary as his main reason for coming to earth. In Mark 10:45, for instance, he explained, '... the Son of Man did not come to be served, but to serve, and to give His life a ransom for many.' John's vivid eyewitness account of Christ's death records Christ taking a drink of vinegar to quench his raging thirst and then exclaiming the triumphant words of an accomplished redemption: 'when Jesus had received the sour wine, He said, "It is finished!" And bowing His head, He gave up His spirit' (John 19:30). He 'was crucified, *dead* and buried'.

THE NATURE OF DEATH

According to the Bible, death has both physical and spiritual facets to it. Scripture teaches that death is God's punishment for sin. 'The soul who sins shall die' (Ezek. 18:20); 'the wages of sin is death' (Rom. 6:23). Death, in the Bible, is actually threefold. It refers to:

• the separation of the soul from the body
• the separation of the soul from God
• eternal separation from God in hell—'the second death' (Rev. 2:11).

Biblically, therefore, death is both physical and spiritual, and at

Calvary, Christ experienced both physical and spiritual death. Bearing the sins of others, he was separated from God the Father and so cried out, 'My God, My God, why have You forsaken Me?' (Matt. 27:46). He died to save his people from spiritual death—the fearful reality termed 'the second death' (Rev. 2:11).

Spiritual death, that is, separation from God, means being separated from the source of all life, light and love. It is the ultimate alienation from which the gospel of reconciliation redeems the lost sinner. The gospel proclaims, 'Christ died for our sins' (1 Cor. 15:3). He died to deal with the sin-barrier which separates us from God, so that by believing in him, we are reconciled to God for time and eternity. In 1 Peter 3:18 we find a succinct explanation of the gospel and its blessed benefits when it states, 'Christ also suffered once for sins, the just for the unjust, that He might bring us to God.'

Paradoxically, Christ's death is a death which saves the believing sinner from death. Christ's death has wrought the death of death! 'The sting of death is sin' (1 Cor. 15:56). But in dealing with our sin at Calvary, Christ has taken away the sting of death for all whose faith is in him. Death, for the Christian, is not to be feared. Because of the death of Christ at Calvary, death, for the Christian, will be the porter which ushers us into the nearer presence of God! John Calvin wrote, 'He [Christ] died in order, by His death, to conquer the death which threatened us, and to swallow it up—that death which otherwise would have swallowed and devoured us all.'[1]

Christ's death, therefore, was a saving death. Christ's death was the very reason for his incarnation. Immortal deity cannot die, hence Christ took upon himself our mortal flesh so that he could die and pay the price for our sins, deliver us from the sting of death, and bestow upon us eternal life. He died that we might live! 'For the wages of sin is death, but the gift of God is eternal life in Christ Jesus our Lord' (Rom. 6:23). It is small wonder, then, that the death of Christ is the theme of ten thousand Christian hymns.

We sing the praise of Him who died,
Of Him who died upon the cross;
The sinner's hope let men deride;
For this we count the world but loss.

Inscribed upon the cross we see
In shining letters, 'God is love':
He bears our sins upon the tree:
He brings us mercy from above.   (Thomas Kelly, 1815)

Was ... buried

Jesus's being 'buried' refers to his being laid lovingly in the tomb of Joseph of Arimathea after his crucifixion. Matthew records how Joseph, after having attained Pilate's consent, took the body of Jesus, 'wrapped it in a clean linen cloth, and laid it in his new tomb which he had hewn out of the rock; and he rolled a large stone against the door of the tomb, and departed' (Matt. 27:59–60). John's Gospel adds a further detail, telling us that Joseph was assisted by Nicodemus the Pharisee in tenderly preparing Jesus's body for burial—binding it with linen cloths and spices 'as the custom of the Jews is to bury' (John 19:40).

Jesus, then, was 'buried'. Technically, he was not so much buried as entombed. The reference to his burial in the Apostles' Creed is there to attest to the reality of his death—he really did die and pay the penalty for our sins in full—and the reality of his resurrection. The same body that was placed in Joseph's tomb also vacated that tomb. The empty tomb and undisturbed grave-clothes are part of the cumulative evidence for Christ's resurrection. The burial of Christ is thus the bridge between Christ's atoning death and his victorious resurrection. John Calvin brings out the spiritual significance of Christ's burial when he says, 'He [Christ] was buried so that we, united to Him by the active power of His death, might be buried with our sin and delivered from the power of the devil and death.'[2]

He descended into hell

We come here to the most solemn and sobering words of the Apostles' Creed—yet they are also words which take us to the heart of the gospel and the meaning of the cross of Christ. Hell, of course, is not a popular subject, and there are many who wish to go in the face of the Bible and deny its reality. Some have purported that Christ's 'descent into hell' in this line is merely a synonym for his burial. This, though, is not the case. If it were, it would not have been included in the Apostles' Creed. The Apostles' Creed is characterized by brevity and succinctness, and it contains no superfluous lines. In a nutshell, this line concerning Christ's descent into hell is teaching us that, when Christ died at Calvary, he actually tasted hell, that we might go at last to heaven.

WHAT IS HELL?

Hell is the place of the eternally damned. Hell is the ultimate in God's judgement against sin. Hell entails being eternally banished from the blessedness of God's presence. Jesus described hell as 'the outer darkness' (Matt. 25:30)—away from the light of God.

Did Jesus really experience hell at Calvary, when he bore our sins and God's judgement upon them? Did he really 'descend into hell'? Yes. He tasted the outer darkness to save us from it. He tasted the outer darkness so that we might bask in God's eternal light. When he died, 'from the sixth hour until the ninth hour there was darkness over all the land' (Matt. 27:45).

Did Jesus really experience hell at Calvary? Was he really separated from God and banished from his blessed presence? Yes. Sin and God can have nothing to do with each other, and at Calvary, Jesus bore our sins and God's just judgement upon them, hence 'about the ninth hour Jesus cried out with a loud voice, saying, "Eli, Eli, lama sabachthani?" that is, "My God, My God, why have You forsaken Me?"' (Matt. 27:46).

At Calvary, Jesus did indeed descend into hell. He endured the darkness to save us from hell's outer darkness. He was divinely punished to procure our divine pardon. He endured divine retribution to gain our divine redemption. He was separated from his Father so that we might be reconciled to God the Father. He experienced hell, so that through faith in him, we might go at last to heaven, saved by his substitutionary sacrifice—'saved by His precious blood' (Alexander, 'There is a Green Hill').

Here is the heart of the Christian gospel. Jesus saves from death and hell. Here is the true meaning of Calvary. He 'was crucified, dead and buried: he descended into hell'. It is truly awful, and yet it is truly wonderful, for his pains have procured our eternal salvation if our faith is in him.

The Holy One did hide His face;
O Christ, 'twas hid from Thee!
Dumb darkness wrapped Thy soul a space,
The darkness due to me.
But now that face of radiant grace
Shines forth in light on me.

Jehovah bade His sword awake;
O Christ, it woke 'gainst Thee!
Thy blood the flaming blade must slake,
Thy heart its sheath must be;
All for my sake, my peace to make,
Now sleeps that sword for me.

(Anne R. Cousin, 1824–1906,
'O Christ, What Burdens Bowed Thy Head!')

Notes

1 **Calvin,** *Truth for all Time*, p. 40.
2 Ibid.

The resurrection of Christ

The third day he rose again from the dead.

Theologians categorize Christ's ministry as our Redeemer as fitting into one of two states: (1) his state of humiliation, and (2) his state of exaltation. So far, in considering Christ's incarnation and crucifixion, we have considered his state of humiliation. As we think about his resurrection and subsequent ascension, session at God's right hand and coming again in glory, we now turn our attention to Christ's state of exaltation: 'Christ's exaltation consisteth in his rising again from the dead on the third day, in ascending up into heaven, in sitting at the right hand of God the Father, and in coming to judge the world at the last day' (*WSC*, Q. 28).

'The Lord is risen indeed' (Luke 24:34)

The Christian faith is founded on Christ's resurrection. The earliest-ever written Christian creed, which delineated the Christian truths 'of first importance' (1 Cor. 15:3, NIV) stated 'that Christ died for our sins according to the Scriptures, and that He was buried, and that He rose again the third day according to the Scriptures' (1 Cor. 15:3–4). So central and vital is Christ's resurrection to Christianity that Paul said, '… if Christ is not risen, then our preaching is empty and your faith is also empty … if Christ is not risen, your faith is futile; you are still in your sins!' (1 Cor. 15:14, 17). The Christian faith, then, stands or falls on the historical reality and actuality of Christ's bodily resurrection on 'the third day'.

The proofs for Christ's resurrection

Christ's conquest of the grave has been described as the most attested fact of history. 'The third day he rose again from the dead.' The four complementary Gospel accounts of Christ's resurrection are clear: the Christ who was crucified on 'Good Friday' and then lovingly buried in Joseph of Arimathea's tomb subsequently rose from the dead on the following 'Easter Sunday'. From the unembellished Gospel records, the evidence is plain and candid that (1) Christ's grave was empty, and (2) the risen Christ was seen, heard and touched.

CHRIST'S GRAVE WAS EMPTY

John's account of the empty tomb of Christ on the first Easter morning is so vivid that it can only have come from the pen of an eyewitness. He relates how he and Peter ran to Christ's tomb having heard from the mouth of Mary Magdalene that something had happened to it. When Peter barged hastily into Christ's tomb and looked, the body of Jesus was not there. Joseph of Arimathea and Nicodemus the Pharisee had previously bound Jesus's lifeless body with grave-clothes. These grave-clothes now lay flat and undisturbed, still following the contours of the Lord's body and head just as they had when they enclosed his corpse. 'Simon Peter ... went into the tomb; and he saw the linen cloths lying there, and the handkerchief that had been around His head, not lying with the linen cloths, but folded together in a place by itself' (John 20:6–7). This was not the work of a callous grave-robber and body-snatcher. The undisturbed grave-clothes, minus Jesus's body, can only be explained by a miracle. Jesus had risen through them. He had risen from the dead! He had vacated his tomb. The stone of the tomb had been rolled away by an angel from heaven, not to let the Lord out but to let the disciples in to see the evidence.

THE RISEN CHRIST WAS SEEN

The actual resurrection appearances of Christ were many and varied—to individuals and to groups, at different times and in different locations. Paul states,

He was seen by Cephas [Peter], then by the twelve. After that He was seen by over five hundred brethren at once, of whom the greater part remain to the present, but some have fallen asleep. After that He was seen by James, then by all the apostles. Then last of all He was seen by me also, as by one born out of due time. (1 Cor. 15:5–8)

Interestingly, the Bible says that the first person to whom the risen Christ appeared was a woman, namely Mary of Magdala (a town on the banks of the Sea of Galilee). 'Now when He rose early on the first day of the week, He appeared first to Mary Magdalene' (Mark 16:9). John goes into further detail. He describes how Mary initially mistook Jesus for the gardener but then recognized him by his voice. In the Middle East of Bible times, women's status was not as high as it is in the West today. Our modern-day 'equal opportunities' industry was many centuries away! Mary Magdalene herself had something of a disreputable past. Had the account of Christ's resurrection been fictitious, no author would have invented his appearing to women in general and Mary Magdalene in particular. The Gospel accounts of Christ's resurrection, then, have a ring of truth about them. The authors were relating it just 'as it happened'.

When the Apostles' Creed states that on 'the third day he rose again from the dead', it is referring to Christ's physical, bodily resurrection, which is contrary to the teaching of those unbelieving liberals who preach and teach some vague 'spiritual resurrection' of Christ along with meaningless phrases such as 'He lives on in his teaching'. Luke, a medical doctor and thus an empirical-evidence-based scientist, particularly notes the risen Christ saying to his frightened disciples, 'Behold My hands and My feet, that it is I Myself. Handle Me and see, for a spirit does not have flesh and bones as you see I have' (Luke 24:39). Dr Luke then goes on to relate Jesus's eating with them. Bodiless spirits do not eat!

Evidence that demands a verdict: cause and effect

The fact that Christ's tomb was empty and that the risen Christ was seen constitutes the direct evidence for the resurrection. Yet there is also the matter of the indirect evidence for Christ's resurrection. The circumstantial evidence cannot be lightly dismissed. Every effect has a cause. Certain effects can only have Christ's resurrection as their cause. Consider the following questions:

- What explains the transformation of the disciples from being frightened—even cowardly—downcast and defeated to being fearless proclaimers of the risen Christ?
- What explains the martyrdom of many of them? Would they have given their lives for a lie?
- What explains the change of the hallowed Sabbath Day from the seventh day of the week to the first day of the week?

- What explains the growth of the Christian church for the last two thousand years? And what explains the millions of people even today who have a personal Christian testimony to the effect that they have encountered the risen Christ and have been transformed by him?

Peter wrote, 'Blessed be the God and Father of our Lord Jesus Christ, who according to His abundant mercy has begotten us again to a living hope through the resurrection of Jesus Christ from the dead' (1 Peter 1:3). John Calvin wrote, 'His resurrection ... is the certain fact, the basis and foundation not only of our resurrection to come, but also of this present resurrection which enables us to live a new sort of life.'[1] Individual Christian testimony can only confess, 'I know that my Redeemer lives' (Job 19:25):

He lives! He lives! Christ Jesus lives today!
He walks with me and talks with me along life's narrow way.
He lives! He lives! Salvation to impart!
You ask me how I know He lives?
He lives within my heart.   (Alfred H. Ackley, 'I Serve a Risen Saviour', 1933)

The pertinence of Christ's resurrection

The uniqueness of the Christian faith stems from the uniqueness of its Founder, the Lord Jesus Christ. Christians affirm—as we have previously seen—the absolute deity of the Lord Jesus Christ. He is the Son of God and God the Son. Christ's conquest of the grave is the final proof in the argument for his deity. He was 'declared to be the Son of God with power, according to the Spirit of holiness, by the resurrection from the dead' (Rom. 1:4). His miraculous resurrection validates his unique claim. Christ claimed, 'I am the resurrection and the life. He who believes in Me, though he may die, he shall live. And whoever lives and believes in Me shall never die' (John 11:25–26). His bodily resurrection proves that the claims Christ made were no idle ones. The Christ of the Bible is still able to reassure his people with the claim, 'Do not be afraid; I am the First and the Last. I am He who lives, and was dead, and behold, I am alive forevermore. Amen. And I have the keys of Hades and of Death' (Rev. 1:17–18).

Christ's resurrection is also proof that his death at Calvary really does have power to save. God the Father's raising of his Son from the dead was his endorsement and expression of pleasure and satisfaction with his Son's sacrificial work. Christ's resurrection assures the believer that his or her sins really are forgiven by virtue of Christ's atoning blood. '[Christ] was delivered up because of our offenses, and was raised because of our justification' (Rom. 4:25). His resurrection, therefore, is both his final validation and our full vindication:

Living, He loved me; dying, He saved me;
Buried, He carried my sins far away;
Rising, He justified, freely for ever:
One day He's coming, oh glorious day! (J. Wilbur Chapman, 1859–1918,
'One Day when Heaven Was Filled with His Praises')

It goes without saying that a dead Saviour is powerless to save. Christ, though, 'is ... able to save to the uttermost those who come to God through Him, since He always lives to make intercession for them' (Heb. 7:25).

Christ's resurrection on the third day is the basis of the Christian's present resurrection: '... that just as Christ was raised from the dead by the glory of the Father, even so we also should walk in newness of life' (Rom. 6:4); '... you were raised with Christ' (Col. 3:1). In this present life, Christ, by his Holy Spirit, has given us new birth. He has bestowed on us new life—the very life of God in our souls. And, paradoxically, just as Jesus has already raised us up to new life, Jesus will yet raise us up to new life. His resurrection is the basis for the believer's promised resurrection. The grave is not the end for us! 'But now Christ is risen from the dead, and has become the firstfruits of those who have fallen asleep. For since by man came death, by Man also came the resurrection of the dead. For as in Adam all die, even so in Christ all shall be made alive' (1 Cor. 15:20–22).

The ultimate Christian hope is not the salvation of the soul, but the resurrection of the body—as we shall see when we consider the line 'I believe in ... the resurrection of the body'. The Christian's expectation and anticipation is that 'the Lord Jesus Christ ... will transform our lowly body that it may be conformed to His glorious body, according to the working by which He is able even to subdue all things to Himself' (Phil. 3:20–21). Our ground for this blessed expectation is Christ's own bodily resurrection: 'if the dead do not rise, then Christ is not risen' (1 Cor. 15:16). 'But now Christ is risen from the dead, and has become the firstfruits of those who have fallen asleep' (1 Cor. 15:20):

Christ is risen, Christ the firstfruits
Of the holy harvest field,
Which will all its full abundance
At His second coming yield;
Then the golden ears of harvest
Will their heads before Him wave,
Ripened by His glorious sunshine,
From the furrows of the grave.   (Christopher Wordsworth, 1807–1885,
                                'Hallelujah! Hallelujah! Heart and Voice to Heaven Raise')

The pre-eminence of Christ's resurrection

The Apostles' Creed was, therefore, careful to delineate the cardinal Christian doctrine of Christ's bodily resurrection. 'The third day he rose again from the dead.' Christ's resurrection is both a historical and a historic fact. We have considered both its reality and its results, its proof and its pertinence. It is surely a fact of history in a category all its own. It is a fact that cannot be denied unless we turn a blind eye to the evidence and are adamant in our unbelief.

Christ's resurrection proves that he is God. Christ's resurrection proves that his death really saves and that our sins really are forgiven if we belong to him. And Christ's resurrection is the basis of his being able to raise us up to new life now and on a coming day. Jesus Christ conquered the grave. Christians are united in their worship of a living, life-giving Saviour who is beyond all comparison.

I know that my Redeemer lives;
What joy the blest assurance gives!
He lives, He lives, who once was dead;
He lives, my everlasting Head.

He lives triumphant from the grave,
He lives eternally to save,
He lives all glorious in the sky,
He lives exalted there on high.

He lives to bless me with His love,
And still He pleads for me above.
He lives to raise me from the grave,
And me eternally to save.

(Samuel Medley, 1775)

Note

1 **Calvin,** *Truth for all Time,* p. 42.

The exaltation and session of Christ

He ascended into heaven, and sitteth at the right hand of God the Father almighty.

Christ's glorious ascension

Forty days after Christ's victorious resurrection, Scripture tells us that he 'was received up into heaven, and sat down at the right hand of God' (Mark 16:19). Luke, in the Acts of the Apostles, goes into greater detail and reports an eyewitness account of Christ's ascension, gained, no doubt, from interviewing the apostles who were present on the occasion. Luke records that 'while they [the disciples] watched, He [the Lord Jesus] was taken up, and a cloud received Him out of their sight. And while they looked steadfastly toward heaven as He went up, behold, two men stood by them in white apparel' (Acts 1:9–10).

Scripture thus teaches that the eternal Son of God both entered and exited his creation supernaturally. Christ's glorious ascension was a unique event which can only be explained supernaturally. Yet, though marvellous, the event is totally congruent with everything else about Christ. The virgin womb, empty tomb, awesome sayings and amazing signs are very much one and in line with a miraculous ascension back to the glory of heaven from which the Saviour came. 'He ascended into heaven ...'

When Christ returned home

Words fail us when we attempt to imagine and describe the triumphant scene of Christ's homecoming. He had descended to earth on a redemption mission and was now returning to heaven triumphantly, having procured the eternal salvation of God's elect. Psalm 24:7–10 seems to give us a prophetic foresight and insight into this scene of triumphant joy when it says,

Lift up your heads, O you gates!
And be lifted up, you everlasting doors!
And the King of glory shall come in.
Who is this King of glory?
The LORD, strong and mighty,
The LORD mighty in battle.
Lift up your heads, O you gates!
Lift up, you everlasting doors!
And the King of glory shall come in.
Who is this King of glory?
The LORD of hosts,
He is the King of glory!

The golden gates are lifted up,
The doors are opened wide;
The King of Glory is gone in
Unto His Father's side.

Thou art gone up before us, Lord,
To make for us a place,
That we may be where now Thou art,
And look upon God's face.   (Cecil Frances Alexander, 1858)

Every major Christian doctrine has its comforting, pastoral implications, and Christ's ascension is no exception. Jesus himself said, 'Let not your heart be troubled; you believe in God, believe also in Me. In My Father's house are many mansions; if it were not so, I would have told you. I go to prepare a place for you' (John 14:1–2). Heaven—'the Father's house'—is a prepared place for a prepared people. By his sacrifice on the cross, Jesus has made his people fit for heaven. Through his ascension into heaven, Jesus is currently making heaven fit for his people! John Calvin comments,

By His ascension into heaven He has opened to us the gate of the kingdom of heaven which was closed to everyone in Adam. In fact He has entered into heaven with our human nature, in our name, as it were, so that in Him we already possess heaven through hope and sit with Him in the heavenly realms. And it is for our good that He has entered God's sanctuary—a sanctuary not made by man's hand ...[1]

'He ascended into heaven ...' Jesus has gone before us. He has paved the way and he is preparing our place. His ascension into heaven tells us that Jesus 'the forerunner has entered [heaven] for us' (Heb. 6:20).

Christ's ascension marks the conclusion of his mission. But going beyond the conclusion of his mission, the Apostles' Creed takes us to Christ's session—to the crowning of his Messiahship and the continuation of his ministry.

The session of Christ

'[He] sitteth at the right hand of God the Father almighty.' 'Jesus Christ', writes Peter, '... has gone into heaven and is at the right hand of God, angels and authorities and powers having been made subject to Him' (1 Peter 3:22). Hebrews 10:12 states similarly that Christ, 'after He had offered one sacrifice for sins forever, sat down at the right hand of God'. The expression 'the right hand of God' is a reference to a place of supreme honour, authority, power and eminence. Jesus was 'for the suffering of death crowned with glory and honor' (Heb. 2:9). God the Father bestowed on his Son the highest honour and accolade. 'He humbled Himself and became obedient to the point of death, even the death of the cross. Therefore God also has highly exalted Him and given Him the name [that is, the rank] which is above every name, that at the name of Jesus every knee should bow' (Phil. 2:8–10). Jesus 'sitteth at the right hand of God the Father almighty':

The head that once was crowned with thorns
Is crowned with glory now;
A royal diadem adorns
The mighty Victor's brow.

The highest place that heaven affords
Is His by sovereign right;
The King of kings and Lord of lords,
And heaven's eternal light.   (Thomas Kelly, 1820)

Christ's session at God's right hand draws our attention to the two realities of: (1) the exalted Kingship of Christ, and (2) the eternal Priesthood of Christ.

THE KINGSHIP OF CHRIST

Jesus reigns! He is 'KING OF KINGS AND LORD OF LORDS' (Rev. 19:16). From his exalted position and place of authority at God's right hand, he rules over all things for the glory of his name and the benefit and blessing of his church—those he died to redeem. God the Father

raised Him from the dead and seated Him at His right hand in the heavenly places, far above all principality and power and might and dominion, and every name that is named, not only in this age but also in that which is to come. And He put all things under His feet, and gave Him to be head over all things to the church.

(Eph. 1:20–22)

There is no higher authority than Christ's. His people may have the utmost confidence in him and in his saving sway over their lives. 'But to the Son He says, "Your throne, O God, is forever and ever; a scepter of righteousness is the scepter of Your kingdom"' (Heb. 1:8). Jesus could say, 'All authority has been given to Me in heaven and on earth' (Matt. 28:18). Christians contend for Christ's crown and covenant. King Jesus will have his way. All creatures will yet own his sway. 'For He must reign till He has put all enemies under His feet' (1 Cor. 15:25).

Jesus's current position, enthroned at God's right hand, therefore reminds us of his Kingship. He is King and actually exercises his Kingship: 'Christ executeth the office of a king, in subduing us to himself, in ruling and defending us, and in restraining and conquering all his and our enemies' (WSC, Q. 26).

THE PRIESTHOOD OF CHRIST

According to Scripture, Christ's exalted session and his eternal Priesthood are co-existent. We turn, then, to Christ's current 'High-Priestly ministry'. At God's right hand, Jesus prays for his own. 'Christ ... is even at the right hand of God, who also makes intercession for us ...' (Rom. 8:34). 'He always lives to make intercession for them' (Heb. 7:25).

Christ's current intercession for his own is one facet of his High-Priestly ministry. The 'job description' of a priest in Old Testament times was to offer sacrifice for sin and to make supplication to God. Christ's High-Priestly ministry has rendered all human priesthood obsolete and redundant. 'Christ executeth the office of a priest, in his once offering up of himself a sacrifice to satisfy divine justice, and reconcile us to God, and in making continual intercession for us' (*WSC*, Q. 25).

At Calvary, Christ offered his own self, once for all, as a sacrifice for sin, and now, by his continual intercession, keeps his people in the benefit of his sacrifice. John wrote, 'if anyone sins, we have an Advocate with the Father, Jesus Christ the righteous' (1 John 2:1). The word 'advocate' is a translation of the Greek word *parakletos*, meaning 'one called alongside to help'. If we belong to Jesus, we have an Advocate with God the Father in heaven. Jesus 'speaks up for us' at God's right hand. He pleads our case by pleading his case—he has fully atoned for our sins, and God the Father accepts us because of Christ's finished work. Christ's sacrifice is complete. Christ's supplication, however, will continue until we are saved to sin no more. In Christ we have a peerless, potent and perpetual Advocate—'a great High Priest who has passed through the heavens, Jesus the Son of God' (Heb. 4:14):

Before the throne of God above
I have a strong, a perfect plea;
A great High Priest whose Name is Love,
Who ever lives and pleads for me.
My name is graven on His hands,
My name is written on His heart.
I know that while in heaven He stands
No tongue can bid me thence depart.

When Satan tempts me to despair
And tells me of the guilt within,
Upward I look and see Him there
Who made an end of all my sin.
Because the sinless Saviour died
My sinful soul is counted free.
For God the just is satisfied
To look on Him and pardon me.

(Charitie L. Bancroft, 1863)

Jesus has 'ascended into heaven, and sitteth at the right hand of God the Father almighty'. Our ascended Saviour is 'risen, ascended, glorified'.[2] He is the King whom we honour and adore. He is our great High Priest who constantly prays for us. Blessed be his Name!

Notes

1 **Calvin,** *Truth for all Time,* p. 42.
2 **George Hugh Bourne,** 1840–1925, 'Lord Enthroned in Heavenly Splendour'.

The second coming of Christ

… From thence he shall come to judge the quick and the dead.

The last-ever recorded words of Christ—and the penultimate verse of the whole Bible—are contained in Revelation 22:20: 'Surely I am coming quickly.' The words remind us that Jesus is coming again. He is coming again personally, physically, visibly, suddenly, triumphantly and gloriously. 'This same Jesus, who was taken up from you into heaven, will so come in like manner as you saw Him go into heaven' (Acts 1:11).

Christ's second coming

According to the Bible, history has a distinct and definite goal. That goal is the second coming of Christ at the end of the age. Jesus is coming again in power and great glory. When he comes again, he will overthrow all evil and all that is incompatible with his reign, and set up God's universal kingdom of righteousness, peace and love. 'From thence [that is, from the Father's right hand in heaven] he [the Lord Jesus] shall come to judge the quick [those alive on earth at his coming] and the dead [everyone who has ever lived and died before his coming].' There are, we are told, some 318 references to Christ's second coming in the New Testament.

While Christians look back to Calvary, where Christ purchased our redemption, they also look forward to better, even glorious times. They look forward to Christ's second coming: 'the blessed hope and glorious appearing of our great God and Savior Jesus Christ' (Titus 2:13). Christ's first coming was characterized by relative obscurity. Though he was the very Son of God, he was born in an outhouse in Bethlehem, and only his earthly parents, some mute animals and some local shepherds were witnesses to his birth. Christ's second coming, however, will be on an altogether different plane. It will be a cosmic event that none can avoid or ignore. 'Behold, He is coming with clouds, and every eye will see Him …' (Rev. 1:7).

The Christian faith is, in some respects, lived in the future tense as well as the present tense. Keeping the future second coming of Christ in mind keeps us from succumbing to discouragement and gives us grace to bear our present afflictions. Christ's second coming is also a powerful incentive for evangelism. Jesus will surely triumph. Better days are yet to come. 'I consider that the sufferings of this present time are not worthy to be compared with the glory which shall be revealed in us' (Rom. 8:18). Our Lord and Saviour will have the last and final say!

Jesus is coming! Sing the glad word!
Coming for those He redeemed by His blood,
Coming to reign as the glorified Lord!
Jesus is coming again! (Daniel W. White, 1894)

There is, however, a sobering and formidable facet to Christ's second coming, for Scripture teaches that when Christ comes again, he will judge the world. This final judgement will, simultaneously, be a time of blessing and of remorse. It will bring in the full and final salvation of all those who belong to Jesus, but will also spell the eternal doom of all those who are outside the sphere of Christ's saving grace.

Christ the Judge

'He shall come to judge the quick and the dead.' This means that Christ will be the universal Judge of all people who have ever lived, whether they are alive on earth or dead at his second coming.

That the Lord Jesus will one day judge the whole universe is and will be yet another evidence of his absolute deity. Absolute judgement belongs only to one with absolute authority. Jesus is thus a Person who cannot be avoided or ignored—even if he is ignored, by many, at the moment. Jesus himself said that 'the Father ... has given Him [the Son] authority to execute judgment also, because He is the Son of Man' (John 5:26–27). Peter preached, 'it is He who was ordained by God to be Judge of the living and the dead' (Acts 10:42). And Paul proclaimed that God 'has appointed a day on which He will judge the world in righteousness by the Man whom He has ordained. He has given assurance of this to all by raising Him from the dead' (Acts 17:31).

We do not normally like the idea of judgement. It unsettles us. We know that human judgement can be flawed and biased … But this Judge is infinitely righteous. And this Judge is our Saviour and Friend. If we belong to him now, and are currently 'justified by His blood' (Rom. 5:9), we need not fear the Last Day, for, guilty sinners though we are, we will be eternally acquitted. The Judge has already borne our sentence at Calvary.

There is, for Christians, paradoxically, a comfort in Christ's final judgement. There is so much injustice in our world. Evil-doers seem to 'get away with it'. But God is a supremely moral God. Righteousness is part of his intrinsic nature. Jesus is coming to judge everyone. He will mete out God's just judgement and put right all that is wrong. John Calvin wrote, 'He will render to all according to their works, just as each one, by his works, will have shown himself to be faithful or unfaithful. It is an extraordinary comfort to us to know that the judgement is committed to the very one whose coming means, for us, nothing but salvation.'[1]

Similarly, the *Heidelberg Catechism* asks the question, 'What comfort is it to thee that "Christ shall come again to judge the quick and the dead"?' (Q. 52). The answer it gives is this:

That in all my sorrows and persecutions, with uplifted head I look for the very same person, who before offered himself for my sake, to the tribunal of God, and has removed all curse from me, to come as judge from heaven: who shall cast all his and my enemies into everlasting condemnation, but shall translate me with all his chosen ones to himself, into heavenly joys and glory.

Judgement Day

Our world, then, is heading inexorably towards divine judgement. And this judgement will be undertaken by the Lord Jesus Christ. It is he who will determine the eternal destiny of everyone, whether that is heaven or hell, eternal bliss or eternal burning. 'For He is coming to judge the earth. With righteousness He shall judge the world, and the peoples with equity' (Ps. 98:9).

Our fear of judgement is a rational one, for God is a just God. Judgement is a corollary of his justice. God can no more not judge sin than he can cease to be God. Our fear of judgement stems from the fact that we know we are sinners before him. 'For there is not a just man on earth who does good and does not sin' (Eccles. 7:20); 'all have sinned and fall short of the glory of God' (Rom. 3:23). Hence the psalmist's desperate cry, 'If You, LORD, should mark iniquities, O Lord, who could stand?' (Ps. 130:3). Judgement is bad news, as we are all condemned sinners in God's sight. Ultimately, all sin is a violation of God's law, a rebellion against Almighty God himself. Hence the seriousness of sin and the gravity of Judgement Day.

While the Bible says that we are all sinners, it also, however, subdivides sinners. Sinners fit into one of two categories: (1) saved sinners, and (2) lost sinners. The division between the two is the redeeming work of Christ on the cross.

THE CHRISTIAN AND THE FINAL JUDGEMENT

Christians are saved sinners. Those whose faith is in the crucified Christ need not fear the final judgement, for at Calvary, Jesus was judged in our place, for our sins, so that we might be eternally exonerated. Christians are sinners, yet Christians are saved sinners. Because of the Calvary work of Christ, the Bible is able to promise, 'There is therefore now no condemnation to those who are in Christ Jesus' (Rom. 8:1). In 1 Thessalonians 5:9 believers are assured that 'God did not appoint us to wrath, but to obtain salvation through our Lord Jesus Christ'. The Christian's sins have already been judged! They were judged in our Saviour-substitute at Calvary, 'who Himself bore our sins in His own body on the tree' (1 Peter 2:24). Our 'boldness in the day of judgment' (1 John 4:17), then, is not in ourselves but in our Saviour. Jesus himself said, 'Most assuredly, I say to you, he who hears My word and believes in Him who sent Me has everlasting life, and shall not come into judgment, but has passed from death into life' (John 5:24). Clothed in Christ's own righteousness, we will be declared righteous at the final judgement. Christ has taken our sin and imputed to us his perfect righteousness. A saving transaction has occurred in our lives. 'For He made Him who knew no sin to be sin for us, that we might become the righteousness of God in Him' (2 Cor. 5:21). The 'gospel of justification' is a solace which this world can neither give nor take away. 'Justification is an act of God's free grace, wherein he pardoneth all our sins, and accepteth us as righteous in his sight, only for the righteousness of Christ imputed to us, and received by faith alone' (*WSC*, Q. 33).

Christians, then, do not fear the Judgement Day. The Judge is our Saviour who died to save us. At the final judgement, he will declare us righteous and usher us into his eternal kingdom of blessing and bliss.

THE CHRISTLESS AND THE FINAL JUDGEMENT

'He shall come to judge the quick and the dead.' Non-Christians have no Saviour from sin. Hence, very sadly and soberingly, they will bear the consequences of their own sin, and bear it eternally. Sin against the eternal God has eternal consequences. John 3:36 tells us, 'He who believes in the Son has everlasting life; and he who does not believe the Son shall not see life, but the wrath of God abides on him.'

As the second coming of Christ will be a time of eternal blessing for the Christian, contrariwise, for the non-Christian, it will be a time of eternal woe. Some of the most sobering and formidable words in the New Testament are contained in 2 Thessalonians 1:7–9. They describe something of the impending horror for the Christless at Christ's second coming, 'when the Lord Jesus is revealed from heaven with His mighty angels, in flaming fire taking vengeance on those who do not know God, and on those who do not obey the gospel of our Lord Jesus Christ. These shall be punished with everlasting destruction from the presence of the Lord and from the glory of His power.'

Paradoxically, Christ is the great Divider of men, as well as the great Reconciler of men. Knowing Christ is the difference, and knowing Christ will be the difference between judgement and justification, heaven and hell, eternal reconciliation to God or eternal separation from God, eternal suffering or eternal salvation: 'The Lord Jesus Christ will return in glory. He will raise the dead and judge the world in righteousness. The wicked will be sent to eternal punishment and the righteous will be welcomed into a life of eternal joy in fellowship with God. God will make all things new and will be glorified forever.'[2]

It is the certainty of Christ's second coming and his subsequent judgement of all which gives great incentive and great urgency to the evangelistic task. Salvation is the most urgent matter there is. 'Believe on the Lord Jesus Christ, and you will be saved' (Acts 16:31). The Bible states categorically, 'Nor is there salvation in any other, for there is no other name under heaven given among men by which we must be saved' (Acts 4:12).

Christ's second coming and final judgement will be the doom of the Christless and the delight of the Christian. On the latter he will bestow new and glorious resurrection bodies, raising us up to a plane of living we have never known before. 'At the resurrection, believers, being raised up in glory, shall be openly acknowledged and acquitted in the day of judgement, and made perfectly blessed in the full enjoying of God to all eternity' (*WSC*, Q. 38).

'"Surely I am coming quickly." Amen. Even so, come, Lord Jesus!' (Rev. 22:20).

Notes

1 **Calvin,** *Truth for all Time*, p. 43.
2 *The Basis of Faith of The Fellowship of Independent Evangelical Churches*, at: fiec.org.uk.

The third Person of the Trinity

I believe in the Holy Ghost.

Christians do indeed 'believe in the Holy Ghost [Spirit]'. This is because Scripture has much to say about both the Person and the Work of God's Holy Spirit, and also because every Christian has been and continues to be a recipient and beneficiary of the Spirit of God's gracious ministry. God imparts his divine grace and blessing to individual human hearts through the blessed agency of his Holy Spirit.

In the upper room, speaking before his impending death, Jesus said, 'I will pray the Father, and He will give you another Helper, that He may abide with you forever—the Spirit of truth ...' (John 14:16–17). He was referring to the third Person of the Trinity, and his prayer was wonderfully answered. In 1 Thessalonians 4:8 Paul writes as a matter of accomplished fact that 'God ... has also given us his Holy Spirit'. The Holy Spirit indwells every Christian. It is he who is the presence of God with us day by day. God specifically dwells with his people by his Holy Spirit—just as he dwelt specifically and particularly in the ancient temple at Jerusalem in times past. 'Do you not know that you are the temple of God and that the Spirit of God dwells in you?' (1 Cor. 3:16).

The Holy Spirit is the third Person of the divine Trinity. We first read of him in the second verse of the Bible, where we are informed that, when God created the universe, 'the Spirit of God was hovering over the face of the waters' (Gen. 1:2). Then, on the very last page of the Bible, a closing invitation to partake of Christ and his salvation is given by none other than that selfsame Spirit of God: 'the Spirit and the bride say, "Come!" And let him who hears say, "Come!" And let him who thirsts come. Whoever desires, let him take the water of life freely' (Rev. 22:17). The Bible itself—God's own revelation—is inexplicable apart from the agency of God's Holy Spirit, for 'All Scripture is given by inspiration of God ...' (2 Tim. 3:16; that is, all Scripture is the product of the out-breathing of God's Holy Spirit). The Holy Spirit's divine superintendence of the human authors of

Scripture accounts for Scripture's inerrancy, for it was he who ensured that the authors wrote the very words of God himself.

The personhood of the Holy Spirit

From Scripture we learn that the Holy Spirit is a Person, not an impersonal force or influence. Paul warns the Ephesians, 'do not grieve the Holy Spirit of God' (Eph. 4:30). Only a person can be grieved. Jesus said that 'the Holy Spirit … will teach you all things' (John 14:26). He thus ascribes intelligence to the Holy Spirit—an attribute of personhood. In 1 Corinthians 12:11 we read that the Holy Spirit gives gifts of ministry to people, to edify the church, 'distributing to each one individually as He wills'. Will, or volition, is an attribute of personhood. Then, in Romans 8:27, Paul explains that the Spirit of God 'makes intercession for the saints according to the will of God'. This intercessory ministry of the Holy Spirit would be inexplicable were he not a Person.

The deity of the Holy Spirit

Scripture teaches not just that the Holy Spirit is a Person, but also that he is a divine Person. He is co-equal with the Father and the Son in the unity of the divine Trinity. The famous Christian benediction goes, 'The grace of the Lord Jesus Christ, and the love of God, and the communion of the Holy Spirit be with you all' (2 Cor. 13:14). Holiness is ultimately an attribute of God alone—'You alone are holy' (Rev. 15:4). All other holiness is derivative from its relationship to God. Here we are dealing with the *Holy* Spirit—the Holy Spirit of the God who is intrinsically holy.

In the formidable incident concerning the death of Ananias and Sapphira in Acts 5, Peter's reprimand to Ananias reads as follows: 'Ananias, why has Satan filled your heart to lie to the Holy Spirit …? You have not lied to men but to God' (Acts 5:3–4). Scripture thus teaches the absolute deity of the Holy Spirit, the third Person of the Trinity. He possesses all the divine attributes—omnipresence (Ps. 139:7), omniscience (1 Cor. 2:10), omnipotence (Zech. 4:6) and eternity (Heb. 9:14).

The ministry of the Holy Spirit

The Holy Spirit of God is self-effacing. He does not draw attention to himself but to the Lord Jesus Christ. Jesus said of the Holy Spirit that 'He will glorify Me' (John 16:14). It is thus doubtful if those ministries and movements that claim to be 'Spirit-led', yet do not give all the glory and prominence to Christ, are actually 'of the Spirit'.

Perhaps the chief ministry of the Holy Spirit—and the main way in which he brings glory to Christ—is in the application of Christ's work of redemption to the human soul, 'the washing of regeneration and renewing of the Holy Spirit' (Titus 3:5). The redemption accomplished by Christ at Calvary is only made effective and actual in a person's life if it is personally applied by the Holy Spirit. We are powerless to save ourselves. Spiritually dead in our sins as we are by birth, we can no more bring about our second birth than we brought about our first birth. Only the Spirit of God can impart Christ's salvation to us. He alone can convict us of our sin and desperate need of Christ, break down all the barriers to saving faith and enable us to trust Christ as our own personal Saviour. Jesus said, 'No one can come to Me unless the Father who sent Me draws him' (John 6:44). Jesus said, 'It is the Spirit who gives life; the flesh profits nothing' (John 6:63). Paul explained, 'no one can say that Jesus is Lord except by the Holy Spirit' (1 Cor. 12:3). We are powerless to bring about our own regeneration. Only the almighty power of God's Holy Spirit working within us can do that.

Salvation, then, according to the Bible, is both accomplished and applied. Salvation, according to the Bible, is distinctly, distinguishingly and definitely the work of the triune God alone. Christians are Christians because they are 'elect according to the foreknowledge of God the Father, in *sanctification of the Spirit*, for obedience and sprinkling of the blood of Jesus Christ' (1 Peter 1:2). Salvation was accomplished by Christ at Calvary, and it is applied to the individual human soul by the personal ministry of the Holy Spirit of God. Thank God that we are not left to our own devices when it comes to the crucial matter of believing in Jesus! The *Westminster Shorter Catechism* is thus very much in line with Scripture when it states,

We are made partakers of the redemption purchased by Christ, by the effectual application of it to us by his Holy Spirit.

The Spirit applieth to us the redemption purchased by Christ, by working faith in us, and thereby uniting us to Christ in our effectual calling.

Effectual calling is the work of God's Spirit, whereby, convincing us of our sin and misery, enlightening our minds in the knowledge of Christ, and renewing our wills, he doth persuade and enable us to embrace Jesus Christ, freely offered to us in the gospel (answers to Qs 29–31).

Thank God for the gracious ministry of his Holy Spirit in saving our souls!

To God the Spirit's Name
Immortal worship give,
Whose new-creating power
Makes the dead sinner live:
His work completes the great design
And fills the soul with joy divine.

(Isaac Watts, 1674–1748,
'We Give Immortal Praise')

The vitality of the Holy Spirit

The Christian life is very much 'life in the Spirit'. The Holy Spirit of God is the very presence of Jesus with us day by day. It is he who fulfils Jesus's promise 'I will not leave you orphans; I will come to you' (John 14:18). John wrote, 'by this we know that He abides in us, by the Spirit whom He has given us' (1 John 3:24).

The Holy Spirit of God is as indispensable to our sanctification as he is to our salvation. Holiness is impossible without the *Holy* Spirit's aid. The Holy Spirit works on both the Christian's character and his or her conduct.

CHRISTIAN CHARACTER

The Holy Spirit brings glory to Christ by enabling Christians to become more like Christ. The Holy Spirit produces the fruit of Christlike character in us: 'the fruit of the Spirit is love, joy, peace, longsuffering, kindness, goodness, faithfulness, gentleness, self-control' (Gal. 5:22–23).

Of course, even the finest Christian will always be plagued by indwelling sin and temptation. Sinless perfection is not attainable in this life. Yet the Holy Spirit enables us to make progress and overcome bad habits and all that is displeasing to God. It is 'by the Spirit you put to death the deeds of the body' (Rom. 8:13), that is, mortify the vices of the sinful nature. The Holy Spirit, then, enables us to become more like Jesus. God is as much concerned with who we are as with what we do—our human being as well as our human doing! He is concerned for our character, and uses various means to conform us more and more to the image of Christ. In a nutshell, God is concerned for our sanctification. 'For this is the will of God, your sanctification' (1 Thes. 4:3). 'Sanctification is the work of God's free grace, whereby we are renewed in the whole man after the image of God, and are enabled more and more to die unto sin, and live unto righteousness' (WSC, Q. 35).

CHRISTIAN CONDUCT

Bible reading and prayer are the two chief Christian private means of grace. When we read the Bible, God speaks to us. When we pray, we speak to God. The Holy Spirit's aid is indispensable in these two Christian duties and delights.

The Holy Spirit helps us understand the Bible. As he wrote the Bible, he is the Bible's best interpreter. The Puritans were right in their emphasis on the necessity of the 'illumination of the Holy Spirit'—'the spirit of wisdom and revelation in the knowledge of Him, the eyes of your understanding being enlightened' (Eph. 1:17–18). We thus pray for the Holy Spirit's illumination when we read the Bible. 'Open my eyes, that I may see wondrous things from Your law' (Ps. 119:18). He is 'the Spirit of truth' (John 15:26); 'when He, the Spirit of truth, has come,' said Jesus, 'He will guide you into all truth' (John 16:13):

Spirit of God, my teacher be,
Showing the things of Christ to me. (Eliza E. Hewitt,
'More about Jesus Would I Know', 1887)

The Holy Spirit helps us pray. Paul exhorts us to be 'praying always with all prayer and supplication *in the Spirit*' (Eph. 6:18). He explains that 'the Spirit also helps in our weaknesses. For we do not know what we should pray for as we ought, but the Spirit Himself makes intercession for us with groanings which cannot be uttered' (Rom. 8:26). Thank God for those times of 'heaven on earth' when the Holy Spirit does aid us in prayer and we are given unusual liberty, sensing that God's presence is near and our prayers have been heard from his throne of grace in heaven!

Finally, we note that the Holy Spirit is indispensable to Christian ministry. He enables us to do what God would have us do, and empowers us for Christian service.

By way of example, consider the apostle Peter. In a moment of cowardice, he denied the Lord Jesus before a servant-girl. Later, though, he became a fearless preacher of the gospel of Christ. The rulers of Israel 'saw the boldness of Peter and John' (Acts 4:13). How do we account for this change? Luke gives us the clue when he writes, 'Then Peter, *filled with the Holy Spirit*, said ... "Rulers of the people and elders of Israel ... by the name of Jesus Christ of Nazareth ..."' (Acts 4:8, 10).

The Holy Spirit, then, equips and empowers us for Christian service. Paul's prayer for the Ephesians was that they be 'strengthened with might through His Spirit in the inner man' (Eph. 3:16). Who knows what God's Holy Spirit can yet do through us? Ordinary Christians are promised the extraordinary aid of the Holy Spirit of God, who 'is able to do exceedingly abundantly above all that we ask or think, according to the power that works in us' (Eph. 3:20).

'I believe in the Holy Ghost.' Every Christian is exhorted to 'be filled with the Spirit' (Eph. 5:18)—to know more and more of the transforming power only he can bring. And he is there for the asking. Jesus said, 'If you then, being evil, know how to give good gifts to your children, how much more will your heavenly Father give the Holy Spirit to those who ask Him!' (Luke 11:13).

Eternal Spirit! We confess
And sing the wonders of Thy grace;
Thy power conveys our blessings down
From God the Father and the Son.

Chapter 8

Enlightened by Thy heavenly ray,
Our shades and darkness turn to day;
Thine inward teachings make us know,
Our danger and our refuge too.

Thy power and glory work within,
And break the chains of reigning sin;
Do our imperious lusts subdue,
And form our wretched hearts anew.   (Isaac Watts, 1674–1748)

The Christian church

I believe in ... the holy catholic church; the communion of saints ...

The divine society

There is a vital, communal and corporate facet to the Christian faith. The creed which begins, 'I believe' also has a line concerning the 'holy catholic church; the communion of saints'. This takes us to the community of those who believe in Jesus. The idea of an isolated Christian is foreign to the New Testament. Of course, individual faith in Christ is absolutely essential, for no one can be saved by proxy. Yet individual faith is not individualistic faith. There is the essential matter of the Christian society—the church.

In the Bible, 'the church' always refers to a people, not a building—for example, 'the church in your house' (Philem. 2). In fact, what we know as 'churches'—specific buildings, purpose-built for Christian worship—did not appear on the scene until after the Christian faith was legalized by Constantine in AD 313.

The word 'church' comes from the Greek *ekklesia*, which means 'the called-out ones'. The Christian church, then, is constructed of those who have heard the call of God in the gospel and have been enabled by God's grace to heed that call and believe in Jesus.

In the Bible, the word 'church' is used in different ways. It can refer to the sum total of Christians throughout the world, or it can refer to a local gathering of believers who meet together in a particular place to hear God's Word, pray, praise and partake of the Christian ordinances of baptism and the Lord's Supper. 'The church' can also refer to the church triumphant in heaven, as well as the church militant on earth. The church on earth in the Bible also has both invisible and visible sides to it. The invisible church consists of true believers, known to God alone. The visible church, though, may contain hypocrites, that is, those who are Christians outwardly but have never been truly born again inwardly. Profession of faith and possession of faith are not necessarily synonymous (see Jesus's 'Parable of the Wheat and the Tares' in Matt. 13:24–30). Sadly, this visible church is also not immune from being infiltrated by false teachers.

Word pictures

The communal and corporate nature of the Christian faith, as manifested in 'the church', can be seen in the various metaphors which the New Testament uses to describe the Christian church.

(1) The church is described as 'the body of Christ' with Christ as its 'head'. 'Now you are the body of Christ, and members individually' (1 Cor. 12:27). The human body is one and yet made up of many parts. Each part of the body has its distinctive role and function to play in relation to the well-being of the whole, and each part of the body is vitally associated with the head, from which it receives its direction. It is the same spiritually, for 'He [Christ] is the head of the body, the church' (Col. 1:18).

(2) The church is described as 'the house of God, which is the church of the living God' (1 Tim. 3:15). The church, then, is God's family. It is a divine household. The church consists of those adopted into God's family by divine grace. 'Brother' and 'sister' describes the relationship of those redeemed by the blood of Christ. A family, of course, is an interdependent unit, not an independent one. It is the same with the church.

(3) The church is described as 'a holy temple in the Lord … a dwelling place of God in the Spirit' (Eph. 2:21–22). Peter describes believers as 'living stones … being built up a spiritual house' (1 Peter 2:5). An isolated Christian is thus akin to an isolated brick! Christians are God's bricks, joined together to make God's temple. This shows that the primary purpose of the church is to manifest the praise and glory of the living God. Ultimately, the Christian society exists for God's glory, not its own welfare.

(4) The church is described as 'the flock of God' (1 Peter 5:2). It has been saved by the sacrifice of Jesus 'the good shepherd' (John 10:11) and is continually cared for and nurtured by him through his appointed under-shepherds or pastors. Any sheep which isolates itself from the safety of God's fold puts itself into spiritual danger. Sheep need the flock, and the flock needs sheep. Hence Hebrews 10:24–25: 'let us consider one another in order to stir up love and good works, not forsaking the

assembling of ourselves together, as is the manner of some, but exhorting one another ...'

I believe in ... the holy catholic church

The church is central in the plan and purpose of God. He has his redeemed people on earth and in heaven. This community transcends the ages and the nations. The affirmation 'I believe in ... the ... church' is made because the ministry of the church is essential to our spiritual welfare. God works through means, and the church is one of the outward means by which God helps us. While Almighty God is not bound by the church, it seems that we are. The church is a Christian necessity as well as a Christian blessing. John Calvin wrote the following:

Our ignorance, laziness and vanity are such that we need a great deal of help to bring us to living faith. We also need to grow in that faith. So God has made sure we have enough encouragement by entrusting His Gospel to the Church. He has appointed pastors and teachers to build up His people (Eph. 4:11) and has given them authority ...

I will begin with the church, the gathering of God's children where they can be helped and fed like babies and then, guided by her motherly care, grow up to manhood in maturity of faith ... For those to whom God is Father, the church must also be mother ... We have to remain under her control until, at death, we become like angels ... Our frailty ensures that we do not leave this school until we have spent our whole lives as pupils ... So abandoning the church is always fatal.[1]

THE APOSTLES' CREED DESCRIBES THE CHURCH AS 'HOLY'

'I believe in ... the holy catholic church.' The word 'holy' here means 'set apart by God for God'. A cognate word in the original Greek is 'saint', which means 'a holy one'. The church, then, is comprised of saints—those set apart by God for God. There is no society which compares with the church, for the church as a collective—as well as Christians as individuals—has been set apart by God for his glory. The church, of course, is a human society. Yet the church, paradoxically, is also a divine society. Only God himself is truly 'holy', hence the holiness of the church is a derivative holiness. It derives from her being the object of God's grace and favour. The 'saints' who compose the church are 'elect according to the foreknowledge of God the Father, in sanctification [that is, being set apart] of the Spirit, for obedience and sprinkling of the blood of Jesus Christ' (1 Peter 1:2). In the next chapter, Peter explains that the Christians who constitute the church 'are a chosen generation, a royal priesthood, a holy nation, His own special people' (1 Peter 2:9).

'Holy' has the connotation of 'special'. The church is special—and altogether different from all other human societies—because Christ died specifically to redeem the church for God. Scripture teaches that Christ's death was for a particular people: 'Christ ... loved the church and gave Himself for her, that He might sanctify [set her apart] and cleanse her with the washing of water by the word' (Eph. 5:25–26). 'Jesus also, that He might sanctify the people with His own blood, suffered outside the gate' (Heb. 13:12).

Chosen by God the Father, redeemed by the blood of Christ, and sanctified and indwelt by the Holy Spirit—the church is indeed a holy society.

THE APOSTLES' CREED DESCRIBES THE CHURCH AS 'CATHOLIC'

'I believe in ... the holy catholic church.' The word 'catholic' means 'universal' (from Greek *kata holos*—according to the whole). It has nothing to do with the city of Rome. The word is a reminder that there is but one church of the Lord Jesus Christ on earth and in heaven. There can only be one church, as there is only one Saviour and only one way of salvation. The unity of the church and the unity of all true believers derives from the vital union with Christ which both have. Christ has his redeemed people all over the world. It was written of him, 'I have set you as a light to the Gentiles, that you should be for salvation to the ends of the earth' (Acts 13:47).

The true, 'catholic' church transcends national and denominational ties. The redeemed in glory—the church triumphant in heaven—comprise 'a great multitude which no one could number, of all nations, tribes, peoples, and tongues' (Rev. 7:9). There can only ever be one true church— 'There is one body and one Spirit, just as you were called in one hope of your calling; one Lord, one faith, one baptism; one God and Father of all, who is above all, and through all, and in you all' (Eph. 4:4–6).

The Apostles' Creed expands on the nature of the true church further when it describes it in terms of:

The communion of saints

The expression 'the communion of saints' expands, defines and clarifies the specific nature of the church and what it is to belong to the 'holy catholic church'. The term refers to 'the fellowship of believers'—the common participation of Christians in the blessings and benefits of Christ. The church is a 'fellowship'—a *koinonia*. Christians have a close, mutual fellowship with God and with one another. They have a shared experience of God's salvation and are in partnership in their zeal for God's greater glory. Bishop J. C. Ryle once wrote the following in an article entitled 'On the Bond of Unity among Believers':

Who, indeed, can describe the pleasure with which the members of Christ's flock do meet each other face to face? They may have been strangers before. They may have lived apart and never been in company; but it is wonderful to observe how soon they seem to understand each other. There seems a thorough oneness of opinion, taste and judgement; so that a man would think they had known each other for years. They seem, indeed, to feel they are servants of one and the same Master, members of the same family, and have been converted by one and the same Spirit. They have one Lord, one faith, one baptism. They have the same trials, the same fears, the same doubts, the same temptations, the same faintings of heart, the same dread of sin, the same sense of unworthiness, the same love of their Saviour. Oh, but there is a mystical union between true believers, which they only know who have experienced it. The world cannot understand it—it is all foolishness to them. But that union does really exist, and a most blessed thing it is; for it is like a little foretaste of heaven.

Beloved, this loving to be together is a special mark of Christ's flock—nor is it strange, if we consider they are walking in the same narrow way and fighting against the same deadly enemies—and never are they so happy as when they are in company. The unconverted know nothing of such happiness.[2]

Putting it poetically, the hymn-writer John Fawcett wrote,

Chapter 9

Blest be the tie that binds
Our hearts in Christian love;
The fellowship of kindred minds
Is like to that above.

Before our Father's throne
We pour our ardent prayers;
Our fears, our hopes, our aims are one,
Our comforts and our cares.
(John Fawcett, 1782)

FELLOWSHIP

'Fellowship' is the word that defines and encapsulates the true Christian church. Fellowship refers to the communion of all those set apart by God's grace for his glory: 'our fellowship is with the Father and with His Son Jesus Christ' (1 John 1:3). Hence the early converts to the faith 'continued steadfastly in the apostles' doctrine and *fellowship*, in the breaking of bread, and in prayers' (Acts 2:42).

UNITY IN DIVERSITY: DIVERSITY IN UNITY

The church of the Lord Jesus Christ is composed of those from many and various backgrounds, yet, in spite of this, Christians know fellowship—communion—with one another. All Christians are united in a common experience of the saving grace of God in Christ which has united them to Christ's body, the church. All Christians are united by a common blood-tie—the redeeming blood of Christ—and hence are able to call each other 'brother' and 'sister'. All Christians are mutually indwelt by the same Holy Spirit of God. All true Christians own, and are under the authority of, God's Word. All true Christians rejoice in God's gospel. All Christians are united in the praise of God; we sing from the same metaphorical hymnbook. And all Christians will one day dwell together in the same eternal home—'the Father's house'. God is our eternal Father. Christ is our blessed Saviour. Glory is our common destination. The church, then, is no ordinary society. No human collective compares with it. It transcends the nations and denominations, and even transcends time itself.

'I believe in … the holy catholic church; the communion of saints.' Those who love the Lord Jesus Christ will also love the church of the Lord Jesus Christ and give visible, physical expression to this faith by associating themselves with a local company of God's people who meet up on the Lord's Day to hear his Word and sing his praise. When we gather with God's people, the Lord Jesus himself actually joins us! He has promised, 'where two or three are gathered together in My name, I am there in the midst of them' (Matt. 18:20).

We love the place, O God,
Wherein Thine honour dwells;
The joy of Thine abode
All earthly joys excels.

It is the house of prayer,
Wherein Thy servants meet;
And Thou, O Lord, art there,
Thy chosen flock to greet.

We love the Word of life,
The Word that tells of peace,
Of comfort in the strife,
And joys that never cease.

We love to sing below
For mercies freely given;
But O we long to know
The triumph-song of heaven!

Lord Jesus, give us grace
On earth to love Thee more,
In heaven to see Thy face,
And with Thy saints adore.   (William Bullock and Henry W. Baker, 1854/1859)

Chapter 9

Notes

1 **John Calvin,** *The Institutes of the Christian Religion* (ed. **Tony Land** and **Hilary Osborne**), Book 4 (London: Hodder and Stoughton, 1986), Chapter 1, paragraphs 1 and 4, pp. 231ff.

2 **Bishop J. C. Ryle,** *On the Bond of Unity among Believers* (Stirling: Drummond's Tract Depot, c. 1900).

Divine forgiveness

I believe in ... the forgiveness of sins

G od's full and free forgiveness of all our sins, by virtue of the death of his Son on the cross, is a basic fundamental of the Christian faith. It is the forgiveness of sins through the shedding of the blood of Christ at Calvary which constitutes the very heart of the Christian gospel and makes it the Good News that it really is.

The forgiveness of sins is a uniquely Christian blessing. 'Blessed is he whose transgression is forgiven, whose sin is covered. Blessed is the man to whom the LORD does not impute iniquity' (Ps. 32:1–2). None of this world's religions can bestow this blessing. Only God in Christ can, for only the blood of Jesus can wipe away our guilty, sinful record and bestow on us a righteousness that fits us for God's presence for all eternity.

The forgiveness of sins is the gospel which the church is mandated to proclaim with a view to the salvation of the sinner. Jesus's final order to his disciples was 'that repentance and remission of sins should be preached in His name to all nations' (Luke 24:47).

The doctrine of divine forgiveness is also, paradoxically, a doctrine to which Christians have need of constant recourse—and will have need of doing so throughout their lives, plagued by indwelling sin as we will be until we reach glory. The knowledge of sins forgiven gives constant fuel to Christian praise. Paul saw the need to remind the Christians at Ephesus, 'In Him we have redemption through His blood, the forgiveness of sins, according to the riches of His grace' (Eph. 1:7). And John, the beloved disciple, with his years of Christian and pastoral experience, still saw the need to pen, 'I write to you, little children, because your sins are forgiven you for His name's sake' (1 John 2:12). Christians can be subject to doubt. Christians often need assurance and reassurance that all is well with their souls. And this the Bible and the Apostles' Creed give: 'I believe in ... the forgiveness of sins.' We are talking here of divine forgiveness. The ground of this forgiveness is not wishful thinking, but simply that 'Christ died for our sins' (1 Cor. 15:3):

He died that we might be forgiven,
He died to make us good,
That we might go at last to heaven,
Saved by His precious blood.   (Cecil Frances Alexander,
                                    'There is a Green Hill Far Away', 1848)

The necessity of forgiveness

We will only appreciate and rejoice in divine forgiveness, and we will only cleave to Christ for forgiveness, if we first realize our deep, desperate and damnable need to be forgiven. And only the Holy Spirit of God can bring this about. He alone can break down all the barriers of self-righteousness, self-satisfaction and complacency.

According to the Bible we are, by nature—as the eighteenth-century theologian and pastor Jonathan Edwards put it—'sinners in the hands of an angry God'. The diagnosis always precedes the cure. Jesus is our great physician, but many suppress their sense of God, guilt and eternity, and deludedly convince themselves that their spiritual condition is such that they have no need of a Saviour. Conscious Christian conversion, however, begins with an experience of a conviction of sin. Jesus himself said to the self-righteous and outwardly respectable and religious, 'Those who are well have no need of a physician, but those who are sick. I did not come to call the righteous, but sinners, to repentance' (Mark 2:17).

The dark background of our human sin precedes the good news of salvation. We need to be forgiven because we are sinners by nature and God is holy by nature. He has no other option than to either punish sin or pardon it justly. Our greatest need is for forgiveness, 'for all have sinned and fall short of the glory of God' (Rom. 3:23). 'If we say that we have no sin, we deceive ourselves, and the truth is not in us' (1 John 1:8). The psalmist asked the rhetorical question, 'If You, LORD, should mark iniquities, O Lord, who could stand?' (Ps. 130:3). All sin, ultimately, is rebellion against and disobedience to God himself. Hence its seriousness. The *Westminster Shorter Catechism* states, 'Sin is any want of conformity unto, or transgression of, the law of God' (Q. 14). It then sets out the consequences of our fallen condition further by saying, 'All mankind by their fall lost communion with God, are under his wrath and curse, and so made liable to all the miseries of this life, to death itself, and to the pains of hell forever' (Q. 19).

Unless our sin is pardoned, therefore, we will spend eternity in hell. The bad news precedes the good news. The Christian gospel, of necessity, has a dark backcloth to it. The good news, though, is that while we have a desperate need for a Saviour, there is a Saviour for our desperate need, for 'Christ Jesus came into the world to save sinners' (1 Tim. 1:15). He came into the world to procure the forgiveness of our sins. And this he did by paying the penalty for them, in our place, at Calvary:

He knew how wicked man had been
And knew that God must punish sin,
So out of pity, Jesus said
He'd bear the punishment instead.

(Ann Gilbert, 1782–1866,
'Jesus who Lived above the Sky')

All Thy sins were laid upon Him;
Jesus bore them on the tree;
God, who knew them, laid them on Him,
And believing, thou art free.

(J. Denham Smith, 1817–1889,
'Rise, My Soul, Behold, 'Tis Jesus')

The reality of forgiveness

We have already seen that in 1 John 2:12, the aged apostle and intimate of Jesus, under the inspiration of the Holy Spirit, saw fit to write, 'I write to you, little children, because your sins are forgiven you for His name's sake'. A literal translation of this verse reads, 'I am writing to you, little children, because your sins have been put away from you and remain permanently forgiven, for the sake of his Name.'

The verb translated 'are forgiven' is in the perfect tense. This refers to a past action with present and abiding consequences. The past action of Christ on the cross, then, has eternally abiding consequences for the believer: the forgiveness of sins. And forgiveness, this verse states, is not based on wishful thinking but is 'for His name's sake', that is, on the authority of the Son of God himself and by virtue of his finished work at Calvary. '[Y]ou shall call His *name* JESUS, for He will save His people from their sins' (Matt. 1:21); 'through His *name*, whoever believes in Him will receive remission of sins' (Acts 10:43).

Technically, the verb translated 'to forgive' means 'to remit'. Forgiveness has to do with 'remission'. 'To remit' means 'to refrain from exacting or inflicting a punishment or debt'.[1] At Calvary, Christ was punished for our sins so that we might be pardoned for our sins. Our sin is so great that we owe God a debt we cannot pay. On the cross, Christ paid a debt he did not owe, to purchase our remission. He paid our sin-debt in full, cancelling it for ever, and thus saving us from having to pay for it ourselves, in hell; 'having canceled the bond which stood against us with its legal demands, this he set aside, nailing it to the cross' (Col. 2:14, RSV). Christ's death, then, was a payment. There was indeed 'no other good enough to pay the price of sin'.[2]

The verb 'to forgive' can also be translated as 'to remove, put away or send away'.[3] Hebrews 9:26 tells us, 'but now, once at the end of the ages, He has appeared to put away sin by the sacrifice of Himself.' In 1 John 3:5 we read, 'you know that He was manifested to take away our sins, and in Him there is no sin.'

The divine scapegoat

A vivid illustration of sins being carried far away used to occur each year in ancient Israel on the annual Day of Atonement. On this day the 'scapegoat' would symbolically carry the people's sins away and put them out of sight. Leviticus 16 describes the ritual involved: 'Aaron shall lay both his hands on the head of the live goat, confess over it all the iniquities of the children of Israel, and all their transgressions, concerning all their sins, putting them on the head of the goat, and shall *send it away* into the wilderness ...' (v. 21). It was all a picture and prefiguration of the Christ who was to come in the fullness of time and take away our sin and condemnation for ever. John the Baptist took one look at Christ and proclaimed, 'Behold! The Lamb of God who takes away the sin of the world!' (John 1:29). Jesus, by

his death on the cross for our sins, is able to take our guilt away. 'I believe in
... the forgiveness of sins.' The forgiveness of sins is, for the believer, a
divine reality procured by the work of Christ on Calvary's cross. Because
of the crucified Christ we can testify that we will never be condemned by
God in hell for our sins. 'As far as the east is from the west, so far has He
removed our transgressions from us' (Ps. 103:12).

My sin— oh the bliss of this glorious thought!
My sin, not in part, but the whole,
Is nailed to the cross, and I bear it no more,
Praise the Lord, praise the Lord, O my soul!   (Horatio G. Spafford,
                                                 'It is Well with My Soul', 1873)

The glory of forgiveness

The joy of sins forgiven is a blessing known only to Christians. When our
sins have been forgiven by God through Christ, all is well with our souls for
time and eternity, and we are filled with lasting joy, praise and
thankfulness to God for his mercy and grace. Divine forgiveness gives a joy
in our hearts, a song on our lips and a leap in our steps. 'It is well, it is well,
with my soul.'4

Sin is our greatest burden. The Christ of Calvary, however, is able to
remove our burden of sin and give us peace with God. John Bunyan was
actually describing normal Christian experience when he related how
Christian was relieved of his burden of sin in *Pilgrim's Progress*. His
burden was taken away at Calvary:

He came at a place somewhat ascending, and upon that place stood a cross, and a little
below, in the bottom, a sepulchre. So I saw in my dream, that just as Christian came up
with the cross, his burden loosed from off his shoulders, and fell from off his back, and
began to tumble, and so continued to do, till it came to the mouth of the sepulchre,
where it fell in and I saw it no more.

Then was Christian glad and lightsome and said with a merry heart, He hath given me
rest by His sorrow and life by His death ... Then Christian gave three leaps for joy and
went on singing:

Chapter 10

Thus far did I come laden with my sin
Nor could aught ease the grief that I was in
Till I came hither: what a place is this!
Must here be the beginning of my bliss?
Must here the burden fall from off my back?
Must here the strings that bound it to me crack?
Blest cross! Blest sepulchre! Blest rather be
The Man that there was put to shame for me![5]

'I believe in … the forgiveness of sins.' 'It is on the foundation of the remission of sins that our salvation is built and stands' (John Calvin).[6] Christians may not always necessarily be good people, but they are a forgiven people. Jesus has wrought our eternal forgiveness—'who Himself bore our sins in His own body on the tree' (1 Peter 2:24). The song of the Christian on earth is in harmony with that of the Christians in heaven: 'To Him who loved us and washed us from our sins in His own blood' (Rev. 1:5). The forgiveness of our sins through the shedding of the precious blood of Christ at Calvary takes us to the very essence of the Christian faith.

Notes

1 *The Reader's Digest Pocket Dictionary* (Oxford: Oxford University Press, 1969).
2 **Cecil F. Alexander,** 'There is a Green Hill Far Away', 1848.
3 Under 'ἀφίημι', **Barclay M. Newman, Jr.,** *Greek–English Dictionary of the New Testament* (Stuttgart: United Bible Societies, 1993).
4 **Horatio G. Spafford,** 'It is Well with My Soul', 1873.
5 **John Bunyan,** *Pilgrim's Progress* (John C. Nimmo, 1895; Edinburgh: Banner of Truth, 1977), pp. 35, 36.
6 **Calvin,** *Truth for all Time*, p. 45.

The Christian's prospect (1): Bodily resurrection

I believe in … the resurrection of the body.

Christian hope

The last two lines of the Apostles' Creed are forward-looking. They are concerned with the Christian's future hope. 'Hope', in the sense that the world uses the word, normally refers to something that is doubtful, uncertain or wished for. 'Hope', in this worldly sense, is an uncertain word: 'I hope that the weather will be fine next week.' 'Hope' in the Christian sense, however, refers to something sure and certain. 'Hope' for the Christian is always a noun, not a verb. The word is part of the Bible's technical, Christian vocabulary. 'Christian hope' refers to a confident expectation and anticipation based on the sure and certain promises of God—'in hope of eternal life which God, who cannot lie, promised before time began, but has in due time manifested His word through preaching' (Titus 1:2–3).

Christians have 'hope' because the God of the Bible is infinitely trustworthy and incapable of not keeping the promises he has made. 'For I know the thoughts that I think toward you, says the LORD, thoughts of peace and not of evil, to give you a future and a hope' (Jer. 29:11). The Bible describes our future hope as 'an anchor of the soul, both sure and steadfast' (Heb. 6:19). God keeps his promises! God's promises of better, glorious days to come keep us stable in an unstable world and prevent our becoming unduly discouraged by the difficulties and setbacks of living in this present, fallen age.

Glorification

The Christian's future hope—that is, the Christian's confident expectation—is delineated in the Apostles' Creed as involving both 'the resurrection of the body' and 'the life everlasting'. The shorthand for both of these is 'glorification'. Paradoxically, even the finest Christian, saved by the grace of God, is not yet fully saved! All Christians are saved and yet all Christians will yet be saved. The final consummation of our salvation still awaits us. This will, according to God's Word, the Bible, see our dwelling in redeemed bodies in a redeemed universe for ever and ever. Salvation, according to the Bible, is one and yet threefold: Christians are saved, Christians are being saved and Christians will yet be saved. The technical terms for this are 'justification', 'sanctification' and 'glorification'. In this chapter, though, our particular interest is 'the resurrection of the body'.

Bodily resurrection

The full-orbed Christian hope is not so much the salvation of the soul but the resurrection of the body. If we belong to Jesus now, we are saved spiritually, but not physically. Our bodies are subject to many mortal ills—sickness, frailty and so on—and will eventually be buried in the ground. Scripture, though, teaches that when Jesus comes again, he will raise us up out of the grave to immortality and bestow on us glorious resurrection bodies, free from all that hinders and handicaps us now in this fallen world. The promise of Jesus to all his own is, 'I will raise him up at the last day' (John 6:44).

Of course, we share in the life of the risen Lord Jesus now if we are Christians. If we belong to Jesus, we have been born again—regenerated. We have experienced a spiritual resurrection foreign to non-Christians. But when Jesus comes again, we are promised a physical resurrection and transformation: 'we ... wait for the Savior, the Lord Jesus Christ, who will transform our lowly body that it may be conformed to His glorious body, according to the working by which He is able even to subdue all things to Himself' (Phil. 3:20–21).

Scripture teaches that there will be a kind of 'order of priority' when the Lord Jesus returns to raise up all his people to new life at the last day. It teaches that the believing dead will be raised first, and then those believers still alive on earth will be suddenly transformed:

For the Lord Himself will descend from heaven with a shout, with the voice of an archangel, and with the trumpet of God. And the dead in Christ will rise first. Then we who are alive and remain shall be caught up together with them in the clouds to meet the Lord in the air. And thus we shall always be with the Lord. (1 Thes. 4:16–17)

What a prospect! Transformed bodies, in the presence of Jesus, for ever!

'For ever with the Lord!'
Amen, so let it be!
Life from the dead is in that word;
'Tis immortality.
Here in the body pent,
Absent from Him I roam,
Yet nightly pitch my moving tent
A day's march nearer home. (James Montgomery, 'For Ever with the Lord', 1835)

'How are the dead raised up? And with what body do they come?' (1 Cor. 15:35)

Scripture teaches that our resurrection bodies will be free from weakness, decay, deterioration and death. They will, paradoxically, be both continuous and discontinuous with our present bodies. We will still be the same 'us', but yet a different 'us'—buried in the ground, but raised up to glory. 'The body is sown in corruption, it is raised in incorruption. It is sown in dishonor, it is raised in glory. It is sown in weakness, it is raised in power. It is sown a natural body, it is raised a spiritual body [that is, a body animated by God's Spirit and suited to living eternally with God]' (1 Cor. 15:42–44).

Here, then, is the ultimate Christian hope: 'the resurrection of the body'. Let us weigh the words of two Johns, an ancient and a modern theologian respectively, to explain this glorious prospect further. John Calvin states,

We are taught to look forward to the coming resurrection. By means of the same power which He used to raise His Son from the dead, it will transpire that the Lord will call out of dust and corruption and into a new life, the flesh of those who will have been touched by death before the great judgement day. Those found alive at that time will pass into a new life and this will happen through a sudden transformation rather than through the ordinary form of death.[1]

Calvin probably had the following verses in mind when he wrote that last sentence: 'Behold, I tell you a mystery: We shall not all sleep, but we shall all be changed—in a moment, in the twinkling of an eye, at the last trumpet. For the trumpet will sound, and the dead will be raised incorruptible, and we shall be changed. For this corruptible must put on incorruption, and this mortal must put on immortality' (1 Cor. 15:51–53). Calvin continues, 'Our resurrection will be such that, raised from corruption into incorruptibility and from mortality into immortality, and being glorified both in one body and soul, the Lord will receive us into eternal blessedness, removed from all possibility of change and corruption.'[2]

Then John Stott, having explained that Christian salvation entails being delivered from judgement to sonship and from self to service, also explains that salvation will entail being freed from decay for glory! Our full and final salvation, he says,

will include 'the redemption of our bodies'. For our bodies share with the whole creation a 'bondage to decay' which makes the creation groan as if in labour and makes *us* groan inwardly as well. We long for our new bodies which will be liberated from physical frailty, a fallen nature and mortality, and for a new universe in which there will be no oppression but only righteousness.[3]

To glorify God and enjoy him for ever

In our new, resurrection bodies, we will be able to love and serve God as we ought, and so fulfil our chief end of glorifying God and enjoying him for ever, free from all that hinders and impedes us from doing this now. 'At the resurrection, believers, being raised up in glory, shall be openly acknowledged and acquitted in the day of judgement, and made perfectly blessed in the full enjoying of God to all eternity' (WSC, Q. 38).

Christians today, then, live in the 'in-between times' of the 'now' and the 'not yet'. We both rejoice in a present salvation and long for a promised salvation to come—the resurrection of our bodies. These resurrection bodies are as certain to be given to us as Christ was raised from the dead. 'But now Christ is risen from the dead, and has become the firstfruits of those who have fallen asleep' (1 Cor. 15:20). Because Christ was raised, we who belong to him will also be raised. Our present joy in Christ is currently tempered by our longing for this fuller joy—the realization of our Christian hope: fellowship with God in redeemed bodies in a redeemed universe: 'we also who have the firstfruits of the Spirit, even we ourselves groan within ourselves, eagerly waiting for the adoption, the redemption of our body' (Rom. 8:23).

Notes

1 **Calvin,** *Truth for all Time,* pp. 46–47.
2 Ibid. p. 47.
3 **John R. W. Stott,** *Christian Mission in the Modern World* (Downers Grove, IL: IVP, 1975), p. 107.

The Christian's prospect (2): Everlasting life

… And the life everlasting. Amen.

Biblical eschatology—that is, the biblical view of the end of the age and the 'last things'—is actually quite simple. The Bible divides 'time' into just two eras: the present age and the age to come. We are concerned in this final chapter with the age to come. In the Bible, various synonyms are used to describe the age to come. These include 'the kingdom of God', 'the kingdom of heaven' and 'everlasting life' or 'eternal life'. In the ministry of Jesus, something of the age to come invaded the present age. Jesus began his ministry by proclaiming, 'The time is fulfilled, and the kingdom of God is at hand. Repent, and believe in the gospel' (Mark 1:15). His works of healing the oppressed in body, mind and soul gave evidence that something of the glorious age to come had indeed invaded the present age, as complete healing—an undoing of all the consequences of the fall—will be one characteristic of the kingdom of heaven.

Jesus came to give us eternal life. He said of himself, 'I have come that they may have life, and that they may have it more abundantly' (John 10:10). Paul mentions 'the life which is life indeed' (1 Tim. 6:19, RSV). The 'life' referred to here is a life in a glorious, new dimension, infinitely different from mere existence and biological life. We are concerned here with eternal life. Eternal life is a life of fellowship with God our Maker. It is an eternal relationship with God which begins in this life but will transcend time, as God himself transcends time. Eternal life is as exquisite in its quality as it is endless in its quantity.

'I believe in … the life everlasting.' This final line of the Apostles' Creed refers to the consummation of the new life—the salvation—which Jesus came to bring. It is speaking of a fellowship with God greater than we have ever known in this age. It is referring to a perfect fellowship with God that will be the satisfaction of all our needs, longings, hopes, aspirations and yearnings. It is referring to fellowship with God, in redeemed bodies, living in a redeemed universe for ever, free from all vestiges of the sin which curses this present age.

The age to come

The Bible teaches that there is an age to come. The present world is not the final world. Jesus will come again. There will be a final resurrection and judgement when he does come. This will result in the everlasting blessedness of all who belong to Jesus, and the everlasting punishment of all who are lost—that is, outside of Christ and his saving grace. Just as the Bible divides time into two categories—this age and the age to come—so the Bible also teaches that the eternal destiny of everyone who has ever lived will be in one of two categories: eternal bliss or eternal burning; eternal life or eternal loss. 'He who believes in the Son has everlasting life; and he who does not believe the Son shall not see life, but the wrath of God abides on him' (John 3:36). 'He who has the Son has life; he who does not have the Son of God does not have life' (1 John 5:12). The *Westminster Confession of Faith* states,

The end of God's appointing this day [the day of the final resurrection and last judgement] is for the manifestation of the glory of His mercy, in the eternal salvation of the elect; and of His justice, in the damnation of the reprobate, who are wicked and disobedient. For then shall the righteous go into everlasting life, and receive that fullness of joy and refreshing, which shall come from the presence of the Lord; but the wicked, who know not God, and obey not the Gospel of Jesus Christ, shall be cast into eternal torments, and be punished with everlasting destruction from the presence of the Lord, and from the glory of His power. (Ch. 33, para. II)

What is 'the life everlasting'?

In a nutshell, 'the life everlasting' refers to the fullness, perfection and consummation of the salvation Jesus came to bring—'that fullness of joy and refreshing, which shall come from the presence of the Lord' (*Westminster Confession*)—and being 'made perfectly blessed in the full enjoying of God to all eternity' (*WSC*, Q. 38). Salvation is all of God's grace. Grace is God's glory begun, and glory will be God's grace consummated.

The Bible says that 'Eye has not seen, nor ear heard, nor have entered into the heart of man the things which God has prepared for those who love Him' (1 Cor. 2:9). Perhaps, then, we should be cautious about talking of the glories of the age to come, tied to this age and the things of earth, time and space as we are at present. The Bible is more concerned with the way to obtain everlasting life than with the details of this everlasting life. The way is Jesus. He said, 'I am the way, the truth, and the life. No one comes to the Father except through Me' (John 14:6).

What will everlasting life be like? It will be greater than we can currently conceive or comprehend! Eternal blessedness, though, cannot be separated from God himself. He is the ever-blessed God and fount of every blessing. 'God hath all life, glory, goodness, blessedness, in and of Himself' (*Westminster Confession*, Ch. 2, para. II). The blessing of God cannot be separated from fellowship with the God of blessing. Keeping God at the centre of our conception of everlasting life will prevent our getting lost in a quagmire of details. Psalm 16:11 reminds us, 'In Your presence is fullness of joy; at Your right hand are pleasures forevermore.' Notwithstanding his neo-orthodox views, Emil Brunner was thus surely right on the mark when he wrote,

If we ask what is this eternal life? What sense is there in thinking about it if we can have no conception of it? the answer is 'It is life *with* God, *in* God, *from* God; life in perfect fellowship.' Therefore it is a life in love, it is love itself. It is a life without the nature of death and of sin, hence without sorrow, pain, anxiety, care, misery. To know this suffices to make one rejoice in eternal life.[1]

Similarly, John Calvin wrote of the everlasting life promised to the believer,

Being glorified both in our body and soul, the Lord will receive us into eternal blessedness, removed from all possibility of change and corruption.

We will have true and complete perfection of life, light and righteousness, seeing that we will be inseparably united to the Lord, Who, like a spring that cannot run dry, contains within Himself all fullness.[2]

Edenic restoration

The 'life everlasting' referred to in this final line of the Apostles' Creed can perhaps be best understood by viewing it in the light of one of the Bible's main overarching themes: the theme of 'Edenic restoration'—that is, God's restoration of the world to the original harmony that it knew before sin entered the scene and spoiled it. When God finished making the world on the sixth day of creation, 'God saw everything that He had made, and indeed it was very good' (Gen. 1:31). No one, however, can say that 'everything is very good' in the world today. Sin has brought disharmony, disruption and death.

The Bible is the account of Paradise Lost and Paradise Restored—and the Lord Jesus Christ is the key to entering Paradise Restored. Our first ancestors, Adam and Eve, once lived in a perfect environment and knew perfect fellowship with God their Maker. Once sin entered the world, though, their fellowship with God was spoiled and a curse was brought on the world, resulting in the environmental disruption which we still experience today. Nature breeds 'thorns and thistles' (Gen. 3:18), and the animal kingdom is 'red in tooth and claw' (Tennyson). The sure Christian hope of 'everlasting life', however, will see God's final undoing of the results of the fall. The fall brought death in its wake—but God, in Christ, as we have seen, will bestow on his people glorious resurrection bodies not subject to death. The fall plunged the world into its current disharmony— but 'we, according to His promise, look for new heavens and a new earth in which righteousness dwells' (2 Peter 3:13). The full and final redemption promised by God will have a cosmic as well as a personal facet to it. The 'change and decay in all around I see'[3] will not always be so, 'because the creation itself also will be delivered from the bondage of corruption [decay] into the glorious liberty of the children of God' (Rom. 8:21).

The world to come

The 'life everlasting', then, will entail enjoying full fellowship with God in redeemed bodies in a redeemed universe. The 'thorns and thistles' which resulted from the fall will be gone for ever, for 'Instead of the thorn shall come up the cypress tree, and instead of the brier shall come up the myrtle tree' (Isa. 55:13). The viscious instincts of animals will also be eradicated, for

The wolf also shall dwell with the lamb,
The leopard shall lie down with the young goat...
The nursing child shall play by the cobra's hole,
And the weaned child shall put his hand in the viper's den.
They shall not hurt nor destroy in all My holy mountain,
For the earth shall be full of the knowledge of the LORD
As the waters cover the sea. (Isa. 11:6, 8–9)

And being freed from the sin both within and without, we will never again know the consequent pain and misery which sin brings. We will be eternally saved, eternally safe and eternally satisfied. Words fail. But according to John's vision of 'the life everlasting' that awaits God's people, it will be akin to one long, glorious honeymoon:

I saw a new heaven and a new earth, for the first heaven and the first earth had passed away. Also there was no more sea. Then I, John, saw the holy city, New Jerusalem, coming down out of heaven from God, prepared as a bride adorned for her husband. And I heard a loud voice from heaven saying, 'Behold, the tabernacle of God is with men, and He will dwell with them, and they shall be His people. God Himself will be with them and be their God. And God will wipe away every tear from their eyes; there shall be no more death, nor sorrow, nor crying. There shall be no more pain, for the former things have passed away.' (Rev. 21:1–4)

The key phrases here give the assurance that 'God Himself will be with them' and 'they shall be His people'. God has his people—his elect, his redeemed. God has his everlasting covenant of grace, the 'signature tune' of which is 'I will be their God and they shall be My people'. If we belong to Jesus now, we are beneficiaries of God's covenant of grace. Jesus said, 'this is My blood of the new covenant, which is shed for many for the remission of sins' (Matt. 26:28). Jesus shed his precious blood of the new covenant so that our sins might be forgiven and we might have peace with God. Yet there is a facet to God's covenant of grace which remains to be fulfilled. It will be fulfilled in the age to come, when God's people will dwell in his nearer presence and know unblemished fellowship with him, unhindered and unhandicapped by all that prevents our realizing this now. The biblical term for this joy is 'eternal life'. 'I believe in … the life everlasting. Amen.' And this life is still attainable for all who reach out to Jesus, for the gospel proclaims that 'God so loved the world that He gave His only begotten Son, that whoever believes in Him should not perish but have everlasting life' (John 3:16).

Jesus Christ: the Giver of everlasting life

Through Jesus, and Jesus alone, sinners may realize their chief end of glorifying God and enjoying him for ever. Through Jesus, sinners may have 'everlasting life'. The future for the believer is as bright as the promises of God in Christ. The blessedness of the life to come is as sure as God's promise. Hence the Bible views it as a fait accompli and puts our future glorification in the past tense: 'Moreover whom He predestined, these He also called; whom He called, these He also justified; and whom He justified, these He also glorified' (Rom. 8:30).

The Apostles' Creed thus ends with the affirmation 'I believe in … the life everlasting. Amen.' 'Amen' means 'It is so'. And it really is so, because God's eternal purposes of bringing blessing to his people and glory to his name cannot be thwarted. 'I know that thou canst do all things, and that no purpose of thine can be thwarted' (Job 42:2, RSV). His covenant of grace cannot be broken. He is God. The Bible affirms that, if we are true Christians, we will know no condemnation from God and no separation from God, for absolutely nothing in the present or the future 'shall be able to separate us from the love of God which is in Christ Jesus our Lord' (Rom. 8:39).

Soli Deo Gloria.

Notes

1 **Emil Brunner** (trans. **John W. Rilling**), *Our Faith* (London: SCM, 1949), p. 121.
2 **Calvin,** *Truth for all Time*, p. 47.
3 **Henry F. Lyte,** 'Abide with Me', 1847.

The Holy Trinity

Glory be to God the Father,
Glory be to God the Son,
Glory be to God the Spirit,
Great Jehovah, Three in One:
Glory, glory, glory, glory,
While eternal ages run!   (Horatius Bonar, 1866)

You will have noticed that the Apostles' Creed is distinctly Trinitarian in its format. The Apostles' Creed has three main divisions: 'I believe in God, the Father … and in Jesus Christ, his only begotten Son … I believe in the Holy Ghost.' The first division is concerned with God the Father, our Creator; the second with God the Son, our Redeemer; and the third with God the Holy Spirit, our Sanctifier. The Apostles' Creed is so constituted because the Christian faith is a Trinitarian faith, both in belief and in practice. The doctrine of the divine Trinity is often regarded as the touchstone of Christian orthodoxy. All false religions, cults and heresies are a denial of the Trinity in some way or other.

The word 'Trinity' is not actually used in the Bible to describe the deity revealed there. Yet the word 'Trinity' is very biblical. Christian theologians coined the word as a way of describing the triune nature of the One who is revealed in the pages of Scripture. Paradoxically, God is one and God is three. The *Westminster Shorter Catechism* reads,

Q. 5: Are there more Gods than one?

A: There is but one only, the living and true God.

Q. 6: How many persons are there in the Godhead?

A: There are three persons in the Godhead: the Father, the Son, and the Holy Ghost; and these three are one God, the same in substance, equal in power and glory.

The unity of God

The unity of God is a basic axiom of Scripture. If the Old Testament has a 'creed' it is Deuteronomy 6:4–5, which affirms, 'Hear, O Israel: the LORD our God, the LORD is one! You shall love the LORD your God with all your heart, with all your soul, and with all your strength.' The faith of the Bible is strictly—even intolerantly—monotheistic. God alone can declare, 'I am God, and there is no other; I am God, and there is none like Me' (Isa. 46:9). It is the strict monotheism of the Old Testament which is the rationale behind the first of the Ten Commandments, in which God states, 'I am the LORD your God … You shall have no other gods before Me' (Exod. 20:2–3). Jeremiah 10:10 declares, 'the LORD is the true God; He is the living God and the everlasting King.' Hence both the seriousness and the folly of idolatry, that is, giving allegiance to anyone or anything other than the one true God.

The tri-unity of God

While the Bible is very strict in its monotheism, it also reveals a distinction of Persons within the one true God—a tri-unity. This is evident from the very first page of Scripture. The Bible begins, 'In the beginning God …' (Gen. 1:1). The word translated 'God' here is the plural word *elohim*. We then get a glimpse of this plurality when we read on and see that 'the Spirit of God was hovering over the face of the waters' (Gen. 1:2) and also that 'God said …' (Gen. 1:3–29). The latter refers to God's Word. John 1:1–18—with its echoes of Genesis 1:1—describes this Word of God as none other than the eternal Son of God, who, in the fullness of time, became man in the Lord Jesus Christ. We thus glimpse both the unity and the trinity of God—his tri-unity/diversity in unity—on the very first page of Scripture. The account of creation in Genesis 1 reaches its climax with the creation of man. The plurality within God's unity is seen in that epochal event when we read that God said, 'Let *Us* make man in *Our* image, according to *Our* likeness' (Gen. 1:26). The first chapter of the Bible tallies with the first chapter of the last book of the Bible, for Revelation 1:4–5 contains the opening greeting, 'Grace to you and peace from Him who is and who was and who is to come, and from the seven Spirits who are before His throne, and from Jesus Christ, the faithful witness, the firstborn from the dead, and the ruler over the kings of the earth.'

The New Testament

It is in the New Testament, however, that the Trinitarian nature of the one true God comes into sharper focus. We see this notably in the baptism of the Lord Jesus by John the Baptist in the river Jordan—an event related by all three synoptic Gospel writers, Matthew, Mark and Luke. Taking Matthew's account as our example, we see that:

- 'Jesus came from Galilee to John at the Jordan to be baptized by him' (Matt. 3:13)—a reference to God the Son, the second Person of the Trinity.
- 'When He had been baptized, Jesus came up immediately from the water; and behold, the heavens were opened to Him, and He saw the Spirit of God descending like a dove and alighting upon Him' (Matt. 3:16)—a reference to God the Holy Spirit, the third Person of the Trinity.
- 'And suddenly a voice came from heaven, saying, "This is My beloved Son, in whom I am well pleased"' (Matt. 3:17)—a reference to God the Father, the first Person of the Trinity.

The divine Trinity is thus seen at the outset of Jesus's ministry, just as it is also seen at its end, when Jesus gave his final 'Great Commission' to his disciples: 'Go therefore and make disciples of all the nations, baptizing them in the name [singular] of the Father and of the Son and of the Holy Spirit' (Matt. 28:19).

Triune salvation

We have seen that the Bible reveals the divine Trinity in action at the creation of the universe, as related in Genesis 1. The universe was created through the action of both God's Word—the Lord Jesus Christ ('All things were made through Him, and without Him nothing was made that was made', John 1:3)—and God's Spirit moving over the face of the waters.

The Bible also reveals that all three members of the Trinity cooperate in the sinner's salvation—the new creation. Each divine Person has his distinct role in the divine economy in achieving the sinner's eternal blessedness. In 1 Peter 1:2, for instance, we read that Christians are 'elect according to the foreknowledge of God the Father, in sanctification of the Spirit, for obedience and sprinkling of the blood of Jesus Christ'. Then

Paul in 2 Thessalonians 2:13 tells the believers in Thessalonica that 'God from the beginning chose you for salvation through sanctification by the Spirit and belief in the truth'. Christian salvation is thus a triune salvation. If we are saved, it is because we have been chosen for salvation by God the Father in eternity past. He then sent his Son to procure our salvation through the shedding of his precious blood on Calvary's cross. The Holy Spirit of God then applies this work of redemption to our hearts, convicting us of our sin and enabling us to trust in the crucified Christ, and so be reconciled to God the Father.

Christian salvation, therefore, is a result of the working of God the Holy Trinity. And Christian experience continues to be triune. Prayer is one of the Christian's highest earthly privileges. While all three members of the Trinity may be invoked, as all three are persons, prayer is usually a matter of coming *to* God the Father *through* God the Son *in the power of* God the Holy Spirit—'For through Him we both have access by one Spirit to the Father' (Eph. 2:18).

Every Christian grace and blessing is therefore a result of the operation of God the Holy Trinity. The Christian faith is Trinitarian in doctrine, practice and experience. Hence it is fitting that public Christian worship has, since the first century, often been concluded by quoting the famous benediction of 2 Corinthians 13:14: 'The grace of the Lord Jesus Christ, and the love of God, and the communion of the Holy Spirit be with you all.'

The Christian faith, then—as revealed in Scripture and defined in the Apostles' Creed—is distinctly, distinctively, distinguishingly and definitely Trinitarian. It is against this touchstone that all counterfeit faiths may be weighed in the balance and found wanting. True Christianity is Trinitarian in its doctrine, salvation, experience and praise:

Almighty God, to Thee
Be endless honours done,
The undivided Three
And the mysterious One:
Where reason fails, with all her powers,
There faith prevails, and love adores.

(Isaac Watts, 1674–1748,
'We Give Immortal Praise')

'I believe ...'

The emphasis in the Apostles' Creed on personal belief—'I believe'—is another example of the way in which the Creed delineates the main tenets of holy Scripture, for, according to the Bible, personal salvation is gained by personal belief:

- '[Abraham] *believed* in the LORD, and He accounted it to him for righteousness' (Gen. 15:6).
- 'He who *believes* in the Son has everlasting life ...' (John 3:36).
- 'Sirs, what must I do to be saved?' '*Believe* on the Lord Jesus Christ, and you will be saved' (Acts 16:30–31).
- '... it pleased God through the foolishness of the message preached to save those who *believe*' (1 Cor. 1:21).
- '... we have *believed* in Christ Jesus, that we might be justified by faith in Christ ...' (Gal. 2:16).
- 'Whoever *believes* that Jesus is the Christ is born of God' (1 John 5:1).

It is also evident from the New Testament that the words 'Christian' and 'believer' are synonymous. In the early days of the Christian church we read that '*believers* were increasingly added to the Lord, multitudes of both men and women' (Acts 5:14), and in an early New Testament epistle we read of 'the word of God, which also effectively works in you who *believe*' (1 Thes. 2:13). What, then, does it mean for a Christian to affirm, 'I believe ...'?

In the Bible, 'to believe', 'to have faith', 'to rely' and 'to trust' are all translations of the same word. To believe in God is therefore to have faith in God—to trust and rely on him and his grace and mercy in Christ, as opposed to relying on our own resources. Salvation is by faith because salvation is by the grace of God in Christ. Faith is the human channel by which we receive God's grace—the empty hand which reaches out and receives God's gracious promises for our eternal welfare. The message of the Bible—the message of the crucified Christ—is that salvation is by God's grace, not human graft; by divine mercy, not human merit; by Christ's work, not ours. It is by believing in the grace of God in the crucified Christ that all the blessings of redemption are made our own.

We are talking here, then, of 'saving faith'. A succinct definition of this is given in the *Westminster Shorter Catechism* in question-and-answer form:

Q. 86: What is faith in Jesus Christ?

A: Faith in Jesus Christ is a saving grace, whereby we receive and rest upon him alone for salvation, as he is offered to us in the gospel.

John 1:12 states, 'as many as received Him [Christ], to them He gave the right to become children of God, to those who *believe* in His name.' To believe in Jesus is the same as receiving Jesus—entrusting the eternal being of our souls to him.

'I believe ...' This emphasis on believing safeguards the central Christian doctrine of salvation by divine grace. A cardinal truth of the New Testament is that of 'justification by faith'—salvation by believing in Jesus. 'Justification by faith' is another way of saying that we are saved by grace—saved by believing or embracing the saving grace of God as revealed in Jesus Christ at Calvary. Hence the judicious use of the words 'I believe' in the Apostles' Creed. The *New Bible Dictionary* clarifies this further under the heading of 'faith', where it states,

Faith is clearly one of the most important concepts in the New Testament. Everywhere it is required and its importance insisted upon. Faith means abandoning all trust in one's own resources. Faith means casting oneself unreservedly on the mercy of God. Faith means laying hold on the promises of God in Christ, relying entirely on the finished work of Christ for salvation, and on the power of the indwelling Holy Spirit of God for daily strength. Faith implies complete reliance on God and full obedience to God.[1]

Note

1 I. H. Marshall, A. R. Millard, J. I. Packer, D. J. Wiseman (eds.), *New Bible Dictionary* (3rd edn.; Leicester: Inter-Varsity Press, 1996), p. 359.

About Day One:

Day One's threefold commitment:

- To be faithful to the Bible, God's inerrant, infallible Word;
- To be relevant to our modern generation;
- To be excellent in our publication standards.

I continue to be thankful for the publications of Day One. They are biblical; they have sound theology; and they are relative to the issues at hand. The material is condensed and manageable while, at the same time, being complete—a challenging balance to find. We are happy in our ministry to make use of these excellent publications.

JOHN MACARTHUR, PASTOR-TEACHER, GRACE COMMUNITY CHURCH, CALIFORNIA

It is a great encouragement to see Day One making such excellent progress. Their publications are always biblical, accessible and attractively produced, with no compromise on quality. Long may their progress continue and increase!

JOHN BLANCHARD, AUTHOR, EVANGELIST AND APOLOGIST

Visit our website for more information and to request a free catalogue of our books.

In the UK: www.dayone.co.uk
In North America: www.dayonebookstore.com

The Gospel in Genesis
From Fig Leaves to Faith

D MARTYN LLOYD-JONES

PAPERBACK, 144 PAGES

978–1–84625–137–5

UK/EUROPE EDITION

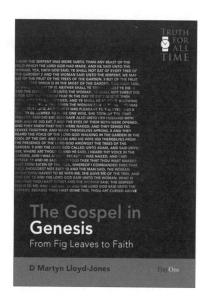

If you've ever asked, 'Why am I the way that I am? Why is life so hard? Is there any hope?' you'll find answers in Martyn Lloyd-Jones's study of Genesis.

In this series of never-before-published sermons, beloved teacher Martyn Lloyd-Jones walks readers through the early chapters of Genesis. The Gospel in Genesis starts with the fall of man and ends with the call of Abram as it examines portions of chapters 3-12. Along the way, Lloyd-Jones talks of serpents and sin, of the Word of God and the Babel of man. But the destination of The Gospel in Genesis is clear: readers will be moved from fig leaves in the garden to faith in the gospel.

Thus Lloyd-Jones preaches the gospel of Jesus Christ from the pages of Genesis. These nine sermons will snap nonbelievers out of their apathy toward God and will embolden believers to share the only gospel that offers answers to life's biggest questions.

Martyn Lloyd-Jones (1899–1981) was minister of Westminster Chapel in London for thirty years. His many books have brought profound spiritual encouragement to millions around the world. His long and profound ministry at Westminster Chapel gave him an influence that was to extend across the world, owing to the number of students who attended the chapel and listened to his sermons. He believed that, even in a secular age, people respond to the uncompromising truth—a view which was confirmed as he saw the liberal churches emptying and the evangelicals maintaining their cause.

Great Gospel Words

COLIN PECKHAM

PAPERBACK, 128 PAGES

978–1–84625–138–2

Here is doctrine made simple! It is easy to read, necessary to grasp and thrilling to experience!

Many people in our churches today do not understand the basic doctrines of salvation. In these important studies, Colin Peckham examines the great gospel words 'repentance', 'justification', 'regeneration' and 'assurance', showing how each aspect is vital in 'salvation' as a whole. Colin Peckham has taught biblical doctrine for years and his expertise in making things understandable, as well as his passion for reaching the lost, are clearly seen here. His emphasis is not merely academic, but brings the challenge of an encounter with the God who made this salvation possible.

As you read this book, you will be instructed and enriched, as well as inspired to worship our great God. It is useful for personal or group study, for those uncertain about their Christian faith, for laymen or preachers to use in teaching or evangelism, and for lovers of God's Word everywhere.

Revd Dr Colin N. Peckham was born in South Africa, where he was engaged in evangelism and Bible college ministry before being appointed Principal of the Faith Mission Bible College in Edinburgh, Scotland. He ministered as Principal for seventeen years. Now, as Principal Emeritus, he lives in Broxburn, near Edinburgh, and has a wide-ranging preaching ministry in Great Britain and abroad. He is author of several books, including Exploring the Bible: Joshua, also published by Day One. He and his wife Mary have three married children and two grandchildren.